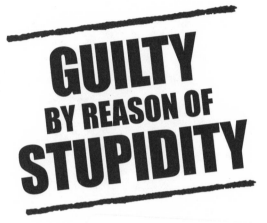

GUILTY
BY REASON OF
STUPIDITY

D1468622

GUILTY
BY REASON OF
STUPIDITY

JOEL J. SEIDEMANN

Andrews McMeel
Publishing, LLC
Kansas City

08 09 10 11 12 MLT 10 9 8 7 6 5 4 3 2 1

ISBN-13: 978-0-7407-7712-7
ISBN-10: 0-7407-7712-2

Library of Congress Control Number: 2008922964

www.andrewsmcmeel.com

Attention: Schools and Businesses
Andrews McMeel books are available at quantity discounts with bulk purchase for educational, business, or sales promotional use. For information, please write to: Special Sales Department, Andrews McMeel Publishing, LLC, 1130 Walnut Street, Kansas City, Missouri 64106.

To my wife and kids, Yael, Jon, and Shelly, who keep me smiling and laughing through the years.

Introduction

As a lawyer, I've had the privilege of watching up close the wheels of our legal system turn. As you might expect, I've seen the good, the bad, and occasionally the ridiculous. The foolishness didn't start or end with the woman who sued McDonald's for serving too-hot coffee (which she spilled on herself after placing the coffee cup between her knees), although in the annals of the absurd that would probably make everyone's top-ten list. The hit parade of junk justice, mentally challenged miscreants, and laughter-invoking legal lunacy marches on.

A teenager gets drunk, decides to walk along the subway tracks to get home faster, and gets hit by a subway car. Who's to blame? Why, the subway conductor, of course. How about a woman who steals a wallet, goes into a bar, and presents the stolen photo ID to the very woman from whom the wallet was stolen? Ever try to sue yourself? It's all in here and it's all true.

I invite you to sit back in the jury box, put your feet up on the railing, and start reading about the main actors in our justice system: plaintiffs, defendants, lawyers, and judges. When you finish the last page, you will reach the only verdict possible: This is the most entertaining legal system in the world!

GUILTY
BY REASON OF
STUPIDITY

Chili con Index Finger

Poor Anna Ayala claimed that she bit down on a finger while eating a bowl of Wendy's chili in San Jose, California, causing her to retch. Ayala went on television and told shocked viewers, "There's no words to describe what I felt. It's sick, it's disgusting. Just knowing there was a human remain in my mouth is tearing me apart inside."

Ayala's story quickly spread around the world, eventually costing Wendy's $2.5 million in lost sales because of the bad publicity. Dozens of workers at the company's northern California franchises were laid off.

There was something suspicious about Ayala's story that both the police and Wendy's tried to put their fingers on: If the story were true, there had to be a Wendy's employee who dealt with the chili who was missing a finger. Wendy's hired private investigators, but no one could find any employee of Wendy's or its chili supplier with a missing digit.

Forensic tests further hinted at fraud. Ayala claimed on television that she bit into the finger. Tests showed she never took a bite. More revealing was the

fact that the chili had been cooked, but tests showed that the finger had not. Details, details.

It didn't take long for Wendy's and the police to determine the real source of the finger in the chili: Anna Ayala. Their investigation revealed that she had a history of filing claims against corporations. Wendy's posted a $100,000 reward for information leading to the location of the finger's owner.

Anyone who had lost a finger around the time of the Wendy's caper instantly became a suspect in the hoax. One could picture unfortunate people in this category searching the country as fugitives, like the famous Dr. Richard Kimble, looking for a four-fingered woman. San Jose police began to get leads from all over the United States about people who lost a finger or knew someone who had.

Since Ayala lived in Las Vegas, Nevada residents with missing digits were the first suspects. Nevada resident Sandy Allman lost part of her middle finger weeks before the chili incident when a spotted leopard she kept at her mobile home bit it off. Doctors at a Las Vegas hospital told her they could not reattach it because of the risk of infection from the animal bite,

and so she left it at the hospital. "What would I want it for?" she wondered. She probably wished she had kept it after being questioned about the Wendy's incident.

Ultimately, police discovered that Ayala's husband, Jaime Plascencia, had obtained the finger from a friend who had lost it in a workplace accident. Oh, to be a fly on the wall when Plascencia explained to his friend why he wanted her severed finger.

This was one scam that had a happy ending, at least for Wendy's. Ayala dropped her lawsuit, and she and her husband pleaded guilty to attempted grand theft and conspiracy to file a false insurance claim. They received jail sentences of nine and twelve years respectively and will undoubtedly long for Wendy's excellent cuisine as they dine on prison food.

The Wendy's hoax became excellent fodder for late-night comedians. David Letterman quipped that Ayala "went back there for lunch today. She's trying to collect all five."

And the country's newspapers, always on the lookout for a clever headline to grab the reader's attention, had a field day. The ten best headlines were:

10.
DINER PUTS A FINGER ON WHAT'S WRONG WITH THE CHILI
—Chicago Sun-Times

9.
FINGER FOOD LEAVES DINER WITH REALLY BAD TASTE; CHILI HAD TOO MUCH OF A HUMAN TOUCH
—Salt Lake Tribune

8.
WENDY'S "FINGER" HAS A CHILI EFFECT ON SALES
—ProFindPages.com

7.
TIPSTERS CALLING WENDY'S ABOUT FINGER IN CHILI
—Los Angeles Times

6.
FINGER IN CHILI NOT GETTING ANY EASIER TO DIGEST
—Chicago Sun-Times

5.
WENDY'S REELING, THE BUTT OF THE JOKE IN BODY PART CAPER
—Sun Herald

4.
POLICE AIMING TO POINT FINGER AT THE OWNER OF MISSING DIGIT
—Winston-Salem Journal

3.
SIX-DIGIT REWARD FOR ORIGIN OF WENDY'S "CHILI FINGER"
—Winnipeg Sun

2.
FINGER IN CHILI STUMPS COPS
—CBS News

1.
WOMAN BITES OFF MORE THAN SHE CAN CHEW
—Montreal Gazette

Taco Bell Burrito Mouse

Ryan Daniel Goff stuffed a dead mouse in his Taco Bell burrito, then complained to a store employee that the burrito tasted "funny." He told the store, "It won't be a good day if the media finds out about this."

But the police learned from Goff's girlfriend that he had purchased frozen mice from a pet store and put one of them in his burrito. Goff got sixteen to thirty months in prison.

Cracker Barrel Mouse Soup

From Newport News, Virginia, comes the tale of Carla Patterson, age thirty-eight, and her twenty-two-year-old son, Ricky Patterson, who demanded $500,000 from Cracker Barrel, claiming there was a mouse in their vegetable soup that they did not order. In what can only be called *Animal Kingdom*'s version of *CSI*, lab tests showed that the mouse had not been cooked and had not drowned; it had died of a fractured skull.

A jury convicted mother and son of conspiracy to commit extortion. Both got one year in jail and had to pay a fine of $2,500.

There is no truth to the rumor that the American Association for Justice (formerly called the American Trial Lawyers Association; name changed to protect the guilty) is selling frozen mice and other goodies to willing litigants.

Here Comes the Judge: How to Go from the Courthouse to the Big House in Five Easy Lessons

The Honorable Donald Thompson, a district court judge in Creek County, Oklahoma, gave new meaning to the common courtroom phrase "All rise," repeated daily by bailiffs as a sign of respect for judges entering a courtroom.

Judge Thompson received a penis pump as a gag gift from a friend for his fiftieth birthday. Lisa Foster, Judge Thompson's court reporter, saw the judge masturbating using the penis pump and watched him apply lotion to his penis on several occasions during later court proceedings and trials. On one of these occasions, she witnessed Judge Thompson shaving underneath his penis with a disposable razor. She did not report this for a period of years for fear of being fired.

Dianna Strickland, the judge's minutes clerk, and Sgt. Michael Reed, a trial witness, later testified to hearing sounds they described as "like a blood pressure cuff sounds [when] you're pumping it up." The noise of this penis pump was so noticeable that jurors at one trial asked Judge Thompson about it. The judge told the jury that he hadn't heard the sound but he would listen for it.

Jury foreperson Helen Orcutt told the *Daily Oklahoman* that the judge was "masturbating, plain and simple. You could see his robe moving back and forth. It was drawing our attention away from what we were supposed to be doing. We all had the same conclusion—he was pumping himself up. You could tell by his gestures." The whooshing noise described by jurors and court employees can be heard on the audiotapes of numerous trials.

Judge Thompson fired Foster the day after she testified before the Council on Judicial Complaints. But it was too late. Forensics investigations proceeded and investigators collected carpet samples, Thompson's robes, and the chair behind his bench. According to

court records, the investigators found semen on one of his robes but not in the courtroom. His state-owned computer had pornography on it.

All these events were too much for Judge Thompson and he resigned in September 2004. In a press conference after his resignation, Judge Thompson denied masturbating on the bench and blamed the chief of police for being the "architect of this treachery." He was eventually charged and convicted of four counts of indecent exposure and sentenced to four years in jail.

The tabloids loved this story; the *New York Post* referred to Judge Thompson as a "gavel-grabbing judge."

"Heads I Win, Tails You Lose"

On June 22, 1979, Judge Alan Friess, a New York City Criminal Court judge, presided over the criminal case of *People v. Louis Santiello.* The complainant, John Haisley, had charged Santiello with harassment. Judge Friess had a unique way of deciding this case. He asked the courtroom spectators to raise their hands if they thought that Haisley or Santiello was telling the truth. He asked Haisley and Santiello if they would agree to go by the vote of the spectators; the defendant, Santiello, agreed but Haisley did not. When the judge asked for the vote, the spectators were split pretty evenly and the judge decided to give the defendant an ACD (adjournment contemplating dismissal), a dismissal that would take place six months hence if the defendant did not get into further trouble.

Three years later, on January 26, 1982, Judge Friess outdid himself in the case of *People v. Jeffrey Jones.* Jones was charged with pickpocketing, and in a conference at the bench, Judge Friess offered the defendant a sentence of thirty days if he pleaded guilty. His lawyer said he would be willing to take twenty

days. The judge asked the defense attorney if he was a gambling man and then put the same question to the defendant. Judge Friess then told the defendant that he would flip a coin to determine if the defendant would get a sentence of twenty days or thirty days. The defendant, no fool, asked the judge if the coin was rigged. The judge assured him that it was not rigged. The judge gave the coin to the defense lawyer, who tossed it and got the lucky side, "tails," which resulted in the lower sentence of twenty.

Judge Friess enlisted other judges to testify for him before a court panel on judicial conduct reviewing his behavior. The panel ordered that Friess should never serve as a judge again.

Solomonic Wisdom in Sentencing: Judges Misplace Compassion

It doesn't take a genius to understand that in the category of crimes, rape is one of the most serious ones. It seems that in 2006, some judges began revealing their lack of judgment where it came to these serious offenses.

Judge Edward Cashman, a Vermont judge, sentenced a child molester to sixty days in jail, so that after this easy sentence, the child molester could get the sex offender treatment he needed. The defendant, Mark Hulett, thirty-four, was convicted of having sexual contact with a girl, beginning when she was six, over a four-year period. After Judge Cashman's sentence became publicized in the media, the jurist "reconsidered" the sixty-day sentence and upped it to a three-year sentence. He claimed that his change of heart was due to the assurances from the department

of corrections that Hulett would receive sex offender treatment in prison. (Yeah, "sex offender treatment," that's the reason he changed the sentence.)

Judge Cashman, age sixty-three, decided to retire effective March 2007, citing the long hours required of judges who have to read cases and issue rulings. (Yeah, long hours and reading cases, that's why he retired.)

A Lincoln, Nebraska, judge, Christine Cecava, gave defendant Richard Thompson, convicted of two felony sexual assault charges, a sentence of up to ten years probation instead of the ten-year jail sentence he could have gotten. The genius reason behind the sentence: Judge Cecava did not believe that the five-foot-one-inch Thompson could survive in prison. The defendant had had sexual contact with a thirteen-year-old.

Drunk Man Cannot Outrun Subway Train: Guess Who Pays?

New Yorker Juan Soto had been drinking one night, consuming six beers and a shot of whiskey over a course of hours. He and his friends went to the subway and, believing the train was not running, walked along a narrow path called the catwalk, which abuts the track. This catwalk was not open to the public. The young men neared the Fortieth Street station and when they saw a train approaching, they decided to race the train into the station since they did not want to miss it. They ran on the track.

Soto's friends beat the train but Soto did not, and his legs had to be amputated below the knee. He sued the City of New York for his injuries, arguing that the motorman should have been able to stop the train without hitting him. The Queens jury bought this argument and awarded him $1.4 million. Lest you believe that the jurors were uneducated dopes not

conversant in the law, have no fear: Two levels of New York appeals courts came to the same decision.

The appellate division affirmed the decision by a 3–2 vote. The court of appeals upheld the decision by a 4–3 vote. The only glimmer of hope were the words of dissenting court of appeals judge Robert Smith, who said the following about Soto's drunken mistake:

I think it is fair to say that [Soto's] injuries were entirely his own fault, even if a non-negligent motorman might have been able to stop the train in time to avoid the accident. Anyone of normal human compassion will sympathize with [Soto]; he is not the only eighteen-year-old who ever acted recklessly, and he has paid a much higher price for it than most. But I do not think that the New York City Transit Authority must compensate him for his loss.

Well said, Judge Smith. A ray of intelligence in a sea of stupidity. New York's *Daily News* put it best: "Have the judges in Albany been hitting the bottle?"

Cops Shoot Fleeing Mugger: City Has to Pay

Bernard McCummings was a mugger who went with two friends to a subway station and choked Mr. Sandusky, a seventy-one-year-old man. Two plain-clothes cops chased the fleeing McCummings and shot him in the back. McCummings was convicted by a New York jury and was sentenced to up to thirty-two months. He then turned around and sued the Metropolitan Transportation Authority (MTA) for the use of excessive force by the police, and guess what? He collected $4.3 million. The trial court had instructed the jury that under New York law the MTA could be held liable for shooting a fleeing felon who "poses no immediate threat of serious physical injury or harm to an officer or others." But the seventy-one-year-old victim had been badly roughed up.

That was not enough for the New York Court of Appeals, which held that the MTA could be held liable because the transit police officer couldn't prove he *knew* the man had been hurt at the time he fired the shots.

As Walter Olson, a member of the Manhattan Institute of Policy Research, commented in the *City Journal*, "In the future, it seems, officers may want to hold off on shooting fleeing muggers until the medical reports come back, confirming that the victims have indeed been hurt."

Judge Bellacosa, a dissenting judge, got it right when he said: "The devastating toll (of this decision) includes shifting the primary concern of law enforcement employees from ensuring the safety of the public to ensuring that they and their municipal employees are not exposed to staggering money judgments, for in effect, doing their jobs of law enforcement. This plaintiff-mugger may have been interrupted and prevented from stealing Sandusky's wallet, but he ultimately makes crime pay by picking the public's pocket for the big score of $4.3 million plus interest."

Will the Juror Who Cut the Cheese Please Rise?

A man was convicted in Brooklyn of attempted robbery and appealed his conviction. His lawyers looked for a mistake made by the court that would entitle the mugger to a new trial. They came up with a doozie: The trial judge had bounced a sworn juror because the other jurors had complained the juror smelled bad and was farting.

The appeals court was faced with the unprecedented legal question of whether the defendant's attempted robbery conviction should be overturned because a sworn juror was discharged by the judge after other jurors complained that the juror had a foul body odor and was flatulent. This was a thorny issue. The First Amendment does guarantee freedom of speech. Was the farting juror merely exercising the right to express his feelings about the case in an unorthodox manner?

On the other hand, the Constitution also prohibits "cruel and unusual punishment." Was the farting juror subjecting the other eleven jurors to cruel and unusual

punishment by farting in the small and uncomfortable jury room? Finally there was the issue of discrimination. The Supreme Court prohibits lawyers from excluding jurors based upon race, religion, or gender. Would the Brooklyn court expand the rule to prohibit the exclusion of jurors based upon the affliction of being a serial farter? Was flatulence a disease to be afforded protection by the Americans with Disabilities Act?

In the end, the court, apparently never having suffered from a flatulent judge cutting the cheese under the robes, said that the lower court made a big boo-boo by not interviewing the farting juror "to determine the exact nature of the problem and whether it could be remedied without unduly delaying the trial." It was a classic example of yet another ivory tower judicial panel unaware of the fact that farters are not capable of being rehabilitated.

What would this panel of five judges do if an attorney, arguing before them, cut the cheese in the middle of his argument? He would likely be held in contempt and disbarred. The five judges would never ask him,

"Why did you fart? Are you perhaps ill? Do you have a medical condition?" The jury was entirely correct in asking the judge to relieve the farter before he relieved himself.

"Court: It's Okay to Falsely Accuse Police"

That's what the headline read on the MSNBC Web site after the U.S. Court of Appeals for the Ninth Circuit struck down a California law criminalizing false accusations against the police. The law originally was enacted after the Rodney King beating case after a ton of complaints were filed against the police. The law punished such behavior with a sentence of up to six months in jail. In one case, the defendant, Darren Chaker, was charged with falsely accusing an El Cajon cop of hitting him in the ribs and twisting his wrist without provocation.

However, the Ninth Circuit struck down the law, noting that false statements made in support of a cop were not criminalized. Of course, it may be that false statements in support of a cop did not appear to be a problem in California. The prosecution asked the U.S. Supreme Court to accept the case and reverse the Ninth Circuit decision, but the Supreme Court refused to consider the case.

Freedom of Speech

In 1994, Matthew Musladin was convicted of killing his ex-wife's fiancé, Tom Studer. Musladin had shot Studer in the back and the head after Studer tried to stop Musladin from attacking the ex-wife. Ninth Circuit judge Steven Reinhardt ordered Musladin released unless he got a new trial. What grave error did the trial court commit to get the conviction tossed? Did it have anything to do with the alleged innocence of defendant Musladin? Not really. The learned judge found the trial was unfair because three members of the deceased's family showed up wearing pictures of the victim. Judge Reinhardt acknowledged that the case did not involve any Supreme Court precedent but that "the wearing of the buttons essentially 'argue' that Studer was the innocent party and that the defendant was necessarily guilty."

This judge ignored the realities of trials. At rape trials, defendants sometimes have a female attorney along with a male attorney. The female attorney will smile at the defendant and touch his arm gently. The subliminal message is obvious: This man isn't dangerous. Some

trials have family members of the defendant in the courtroom. The defendant smiles at them. They look lovingly back. This is a form of support that is not and should not be prohibited in a public courtroom. In murder cases, the victim's family often testifies, even if just to identify the body of the victim. Many times there are crying members of the deceased's family. These events do not result in reversals. More inflammatory than the buttons worn in this case are the photographs of the deceased that are routinely introduced into evidence at a murder trial. If the jury can be fair in spite of these (and I believe they can), what is the big deal with a couple of buttons?

Particularly distressing to victims' rights groups was the fact that Reinhardt used quote marks around the word "victim" in his Musladin ruling. He said the case posed the issue of "when spectators are permitted to wear buttons depicting the 'victim.'" (A revised version of his ruling does not include such references.)

"That was very troubling," said Meg Garvin, a program director at the National Crime Victim Law Institute in Portland, Oregon. "There is no dispute that someone was shot and died."

In December 2006, the U.S. Supreme Court reversed the Ninth Circuit's decision. In the preceding Supreme Court term, the court reversed fifteen of the eighteen cases that had originated in the Ninth Circuit.

Florida Thief: I Shoplifted Because I Am Full of S—t

Helen Gallo of Clearwater, Florida, was arrested for shoplifting at a Cape Coral grocery store. She had a unique excuse for the cops who locked her up: She could not wait in line because she had irritable bowel syndrome.

She was charged with petit larceny and released on five-hundred-dollar bond. This will be a first: A jury may acquit the lady only if they agree with her that she was full of s—t at the time of the crime.

Freedom to Think

A New Mexico judge made people wonder who was crazier—the judge or the complainant. A Santa Fe woman, Colleen Nestler, claimed in a six-page letter to the court that in 1993 David Letterman had used code words and "eye expressions" to convey his desires for her and invite her back east. She claimed that on one *Late Show* episode, he said "Marry me, Oprah," and Oprah was, of course, a code name for her. Nestler responded by sending Letterman "thoughts of love," but she also claimed that Letterman's behavior (or perhaps thoughts) had caused mental cruelty and sleep deprivation and forced her into bankruptcy.

The New Mexico judge, obviously with the uncanny ability to separate the wheat from the chaff, signed a temporary restraining order (rather than going out on a limb by dismissing the lawsuit and getting his court officers to take Nestler to a suitable rubber room) that ordered Letterman to stay at least three feet away from Nestler and not "think of me, and release me from his mental harassment and hammering."

Ginny Wilson, a Santa Fe representative for the National Alliance for the Mentally Ill, said she was particularly concerned that by signing the restraining order, Judge Daniel Sanchez had dragged a person into the public eye who may not be capable of handling the situation. "It's really, really sad," Wilson said in an interview. "Those words she used—it would seem she is in considerable trouble."

A couple of weeks after Judge Sanchez signed the order, he reversed himself because Nestler told him (can you believe it?) that she could not prove her allegations. Nonetheless, Nestler told the judge that if Letterman or his representatives came near her, she would break their legs. Even after Judge Sanchez's reversal, Nestler sounded as if she won. She said, "I have achieved my purpose. The public knows that the man can't come near me."

HOV Agita

Whoever came up with the idea for HOV (high-occupancy vehicle) lanes probably never anticipated the lengths to which people would go to avoid the rule. On a purely theoretical basis, there was some sense to the rule: Let's reduce traffic and pollution by setting aside a lane dedicated to people traveling in groups, as opposed to solitary drivers. This lane will move quicker than the others and will reward environmentalists who carpool. Very laudable. Some states have since concluded that the lanes do not alleviate traffic congestion or improve air quality.

But whatever the merits of HOV lanes, they have become part of our culture in certain parts of the country. The HBO show *Curb Your Enthusiasm* had one episode where star Larry David hired a prostitute whose sole job was to occupy the passenger seat of his car as he drove to a Dodgers game in an HOV lane.

It should not be surprising that the California Highway Patrol, ever vigilant to enforce the HOV restrictions, has become adept at spotting HOV impostors. California cop Will Thompson stands on his car

door rail, which allows him to look down into passing vehicles. One day he saw a vehicle driving in the HOV lane with a kickboxing dummy in the passenger seat. It wasn't the Miami Dolphins windbreaker that drew the officer's attention to the dummy, nor was it the dummy's baseball cap. It was the fact that the dummy who was driving the car didn't give his passenger any legs.

In the end, Kevin Morgan of Petaluma, California, got a $351 ticket for his antics. Morgan asked Officer Thompson, "Well, that didn't help me much, did it?" Officer Thompson agreed, and placed the dummy on a freeway shoulder as a deterrent to others who might try the stunt.

In the Denver suburb of Westminster, Colorado, municipal court judge John Stipech sentenced Greg Pringle for trying a similar dummy scam to spend four one-hour sessions standing on a major roadway in Westminster, holding a sign that read: "The HOV Lane Is Not for Dummies." Stipech also said Pringle could bring Tillie, the ten-dollar mannequin he constructed to earn him access to the fast-moving HOV lane on U.S. 36, with him as he served out his sentence.

Right to Life or Right to Wiggle Out of Traffic Ticket?

When it comes to the HOV wars, you have to hand it to Arizona resident Candace Dickinson, who tried to fight her $367 ticket for driving solo in the HOV lane. When Dickinson was pulled over in an HOV lane by Sgt. Dave Norton of the Phoenix Police Department, he asked her how many people were in the car. Dickinson pointed to her pregnant stomach and said, "Two."

Dickinson argued to Phoenix Municipal Court judge Dennis Freeman that since she was pregnant she was justified in driving in the HOV lane. Arizona traffic laws do not define what a person is, so why couldn't you count the child inside her womb? The court ruled that unborn children don't count when it comes to carpool lanes.

Although Dickinson lost her battle in this case, she should consider applying to law school; she may very well have a promising legal career in her future.

More Traffic Trouble

Jason Niccum of Longmont, Colorado, thought he had the perfect way to avoid showing up late for work every day, and it wasn't an alarm clock. For $100, Niccum bought a device called an Opticon on eBay. Firefighters use this strobelike apparatus to change traffic signals when responding to emergencies. City traffic engineers began to notice that a white Ford pickup always seemed to have the green light whenever a light pattern was disrupted. Niccum got a $50 ticket, and city traffic engineers figured out a way to jam all unauthorized light-changing devices.

She Did Not Want to Pay Those Tickets

Some people go to all sorts of extremes to avoid paying traffic tickets. Kimberly Du of Des Moines, Iowa, was such a person. Du faked her own obituary and sent a forged letter allegedly signed by her mother to a Polk County judge stating that she was dead. The obituary was made to look like a page of the *Des Moines Register*'s Web site and it stated that Du had died in a car accident.

Unfortunately, Du forgot one important aspect of faking one's death: Dead people don't get traffic tickets. She was stopped by the police for speeding one month after the obituary was dated. Instead of being charged with simple misdemeanors, Du now faced a class D felony, a possible five-year jail term, and a $500 fine. Du's defense to these charges is obvious: She was, in fact, dead. Brain dead.

Du got a two-year (suspended) prison sentence, two years of probation, and a $500 fine.

Pedestrian Struck by Vehicle Gets Jaywalking Ticket

Washington, D.C., police apparently have no criminals to catch, otherwise they wouldn't be focusing on jaywalkers. The jaywalker in question, seventy-three-year-old Charles Atherton, was former secretary of the U.S. Commission of Fine Arts and oversaw the design of major monuments and federal buildings. Atherton was hit by a car and sent hurling through the air as he crossed a busy Washington street. He ended up bleeding from the nose and head after being smashed into the windshield.

Before paramedics rushed him to the hospital, the D.C. police decided to leap into action, issuing him a ticket for jaywalking. Obviously, Atherton was in no condition to receive the ticket. According to eyewitness Michael Baker, Atherton was having trouble breathing and could not respond when they pinched his hand. His family found the ticket when they visited him in George Washington University Hospital.

Lt. John Kutniewsky of the police department's major crash unit explained the unique ticket: "He was issued a ticket because he was at fault. That's all I can tell you."

"Do Not Cast Me Off in Old Age; When My Strength Fails, Do Not Forsake Me"

(Psalms 71:9)

The same good judgment that motivated D.C. police was exhibited by the LAPD when they ticketed eighty-two-year-old Mayvis Coyle. Coyle claimed that she started crossing the street when the light was in her favor but did not make it to the other side in the twelve seconds allotted because of heavy groceries. Coyle was fined $114. Because of the bad press that resulted from the ticket, a city councilman suggested that transportation officials make the lights around senior housing apartments longer.

Man Sues Himself for Vehicle Damage

Curtis Gokey, a city employee of Lodi, California, may not have been a lawyer, but he had a good feel for the American legal system. When a dump truck backed into his car, he sued the City of Lodi for damages.

There was only one minor problem: He was the one driving the dump truck that backed into his car. Admitting that he caused the crash, Gokey nevertheless sued for $3,500. (Here a legal education might have helped; he could have blamed the accident on some psychological disorder from childhood.) After the city denied his claim because he was essentially suing himself, Gokey sued the city in his wife's name. Rhonda Gokey, the genius who married Curtis, sued for $4,800, a full $1,300 more than her husband. "I'm not as nice as my husband is," she said.

City attorney Steve Schwabauer took the case. He pointed out that Rhonda Gokey can't sue her husband under California law.

"You can sue your spouse for divorce, but you can't sue your spouse for negligence," Schwabauer said. "They're a married couple under California law. They're one entity. It's damage to community property." All that legalese. I would have just said, "The guy hit his own car. No need to get into community property, whatever that is."

Compulsive Gambler Sues Drug Company

Max Wells, a retired doctor, managed to lose $14 million in the casinos. This fifty-five-year-old doctor wants his money back. He claims he is not at fault for the gambling debts. It is the fault of GlaxoSmithKline, a drug company, since the prescription drugs he was taking for his Parkinson's disease caused his compulsive gambling.

He has the famous Mayo Clinic to back him up, quoting a 2005 study that says that eleven Parkinson's patients developed gambling habits while taking GlaxoSmithKline's Requip or Mirapex, a similar drug from another company. According to this study, the compulsive gambling stopped when the drugs were discontinued. Dr. Wells also sued the casinos, saying they should have known about the Mayo study. Wells had been an occasional gambler before taking the medication. According to Wells's lawyer, when he stopped taking the drug, his gambling compulsion stopped. (It

had nothing to do with his wife discovering the gambling debt and threatening to kill him.)

Prediction: Viagra will one day be blamed for men cheating on their wives by going to high-class hookers. You heard it here first.

The iPod Is Too Loud and Steve Jobs Has to Pay

John Kiel Patterson of Louisiana, one of millions of iPod owners, tried to find a way to ride the iPod gravy train by filing a class-action suit against Apple computers. His unique claim: The iPod is defective because the 130-decibel volume that the iPod is currently capable of playing can permanently damage a person's ear. Patterson complained that the iPod manual did not provide sufficient warning of this hearing-loss danger, even though iPod players are accompanied by a warning that if the units are played on high volume, permanent hearing loss can occur.

No one really asked Patterson that brilliant question: Why don't you just lower the volume? The level of individual responsibility in turning the click wheel is hardly overwhelming to members of the American public.

Apple leapt into action; who needs the American Association for Justice barking and nipping at your heels? They came up with software that was freely downloadable designed to limit the maximum volume

on the unit. It is really a case of "Since you are not smart enough to limit the maximum volume, I will do it for you."

What's next? Will there be refrigerators that automatically lock after you open the door a certain number of times? Can supermarkets be liable for obesity because of the products offered? What about bakeries and ice cream parlors? Cold Stone Creamery beware: You are next.

Finger Lickin', Artery-Clogging Good

Are there people out there who mistake Kentucky Fried Chicken for a vegan health-food restaurant? Who knows? In a lawsuit sponsored by the Center for Science in the Public Interest, Dr. Arthur Hoyte sued Kentucky Fried Chicken to try to prevent the colonel from using partially hydrogenated oil in its chicken and other dishes. The plaintiff seeks class-action status. What does that mean in plain English? That means that if the lawsuit is successful, some law firm will make millions of dollars and each party to the class action will get a quarter.

The Center for Science in the Public Interest, a Washington-based organization, became known as the "food police" in the 1990s when it declared fettuccine Alfredo "a heart attack on a plate" and publicized the fat, calorie, and sodium content of Italian food and other popular ethnic cuisines. Dunkin' Donuts and Denny's are potential targets for future litigation, says the plaintiff.

To me, the issue is not whether partially hydrogenated oil is good for you (it is not), it is whether we allow people to make choices. Ironically, the lead plaintiff in this lawsuit was a retired physician. He claimed he did not know about the partially hydrogenated oil in Kentucky Fried Chicken's food. Thank God he is retired. Here is a doctor you should avoid. He had no sense that Kentucky Fried Chicken may be unhealthy. There was no hint in the title of the food. Arthur, please, pay attention: Kentucky *Fried* Chicken. The word "Fried" did not give him the slightest hint that he might be better off trying a healthy salad at Moosewood. He is like the smoking plaintiffs who, after four decades of warnings, did not realize that smoking is not good for you.

On May 2, 2007, Federal District Court Judge James Robertson, expressing skepticism that the good doctor did not know what he was eating when he went to a restaurant that served *fried* chicken and french *fries*, dismissed the lawsuit because he found that the doctor had not alleged any injury from eating at KFC.

THANK GOD THEY'RE SO STUPID

Crack Purchaser in Florida Worries About Consumer Fraud: Cops Reassure Him, It's Crack and You're Busted

A security worker for MacDill Air Force Base approached two uniformed cops in Tampa, Florida, and asked them to test his crack pipe. He doubted that he had been sold actual crack cocaine and wanted the two officers to test it for him.

This turned out to be a good news–bad news situation. The good news is that the man had not been defrauded; it was, in fact, crack cocaine. The bad news is that after the residue in the pipe tested positive for cocaine, the man was arrested and taken to jail.

The AP headline said it best: "Uh, Officer, Is This Really Crack I Bought?"

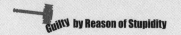

Counterfeiter with a Problem:
The Bill Looked Great But ...

Who says the Feds can't catch criminals? On March 15, 2006, U.S. Customs agents stopped a counterfeiter dead in his tracks. It wasn't the quality of the counterfeit. It looked real enough. There was one tiny flaw: The counterfeiter had created a one-billion-dollar bill. Guess what? There is no such thing. Tekle Zigetta was charged with this genius crime. The burning question remains, Where was he going to use it? Was he going to pull up to the drive-though window at a McDonald's and ask, "Can you break this? I don't got anything smaller."

If I Didn't Have Bad Luck,
I'd Have No Luck at All

On February 5, 1990, a thirty-three-year-old man named David Zaback walked in to rob H & J Leather and Firearms Ltd. in Renton, Washington. Zaback did

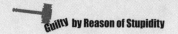

not notice the police car parked in front of the store. He walked in, announced the stickup, and threatened to shoot anyone who got in his way. The cop and the armed clerk ordered Zaback to drop his gun. Zaback shot at them and missed; the cop and the clerk shot at Zaback four times and killed him.

It takes a certain genius to try to rob a gun store, thinking the clerks and customers would be harmless and unarmed.

Cheech and Chong Go to KFC

Two men with a case of the munchies pulled up to a drive-through window at a KFC restaurant in Buffalo, New York, and asked for the Wednesday special. As they ordered, they smoked what the cops eating inside the restaurant described as "the biggest marijuana cigar you ever saw." The cloud of marijuana smoke wafted into the restaurant drawing the attention of the dining cops, who went out and arrested twenty-three-year-old Charles Morris and twenty-six-year-

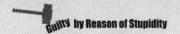

old Gregory Quick. There was some good news for the Cheech and Chong pair: One of the two cops got the cashier to refund the pot smokers' money for the Wednesday special.

If You're Gonna Rob in Ladies' Clothing, Shave First

After robbing a California gas station, an unshaven man wearing a black evening gown, fishnet stockings, a black wig, and calf-high boots got arrested when his stockings got caught in the car door. He had robbed the gas station and, of course, had placed the $290 in cash in his black purse. The Monterey, California, cops spotted a black Saab with fishnet panty hose hanging from the driver's door, dragging on the ground. The police pulled the car over and arrested Michael Leslie Clouse. Lt. Phil Penko said, "I've been with the department for twenty-two years, and this is the first time I've ever heard of this happening anywhere here."

What was the radio call? "Be on the lookout for a black Saab with a person in a black evening gown, fishnet stockings, calf-high boots, and a beard and mustache. Wanted for robbery in the past."

Horseplay: "Wilbur, Not Tonight, I Have a Headache"

From Seattle, Washington, comes the story of James Michael Taft, age fifty-four, who pleaded guilty to entering a barn without the owner's permission. It sounds like a straightforward, trivial crime until you hear the details.

Taft admitted to police that he entered the barn, along with his friend Kenneth Pinyan, to videotape Pinyan having sex with a horse. Pinyan later died as a result of internal injuries suffered when having sex with the horse.

Taft pleaded guilty to trespassing, got a one-year suspended sentence, a three-hundred-dollar fine, eight hours of community service (presumably not involving cleaning the barn), and was ordered to keep away from his neighbors.

The prosecutors did not charge Taft with animal cruelty, since there was no evidence that the animal was hurt. You gotta wonder what possessed these fellas to do this. No doubt the video was played at the police precinct a couple of times. If the horse could only talk like Mr. Ed . . .

More Horseplay

Apparently, this kind of horseplay is not unusual. St. Gabriel, Louisiana, police chief Kevin Ambeau released a surveillance tape showing a young man having sex with a small horse. The owners of the barn had found sexual paraphernalia in the horse stall two months prior and had set up two cameras to catch the bugger. The man in question always went to the same horse. After broadcasting a photo of the man, the police arrested a juvenile and were seeking psychiatric help for him. If convicted, the suspect would face a fine of up to two thousand dollars and up to five years in prison.

Man's Horticulture Skills Go to Pot

A Statesboro, Georgia, man was so proud of his pot plants that he took pictures of them. He had his film developed at a local store and a photo lab tech dropped a dime on him. Byron Charles Mattheeussen faces a number of drug charges, including manufacturing marijuana. Statesboro police found more than forty suspected pot plants growing in and around the man's home. Why Mattheeussen took the photos is unclear. Perhaps he was writing an article on pot growing for *Better Homes and Gardens.*

Videotaping of Sadomasochistic Dungeon

Three Charlotte, North Carolina, men were arrested for castrating willing participants in a sadomasochistic dungeon in a rural house. None of the defendants were doctors. When the police searched the house, they found scalpels, sutures, bandages, anesthetic, and artificial replacement testicles. They also found video equipment. Photos and videos were featured on a locally produced sadomasochistic Web site.

The three faced charges for castration without malice (although to a normal man, every castration would have to be done with malice) and performing medical acts without a license. Some of the victims may have come from as far as South America. "This right here beats anything I have ever seen," Sheriff Tom Alexander told the *Asheville Citizen-Times.*

TV Crew Films Assault

If you decide to assault someone, you should not record the crime. It makes the job of the police so much easier. Rafael Gutierrez Jr. sent the Warner Bros. show *Cheaters* films of his wife, Maria, having sex with a police captain in an unmarked car on three occasions. Gutierrez confronted his wife about her alleged affair outside her workplace with the *Cheaters* crew in tow.

Gutierrez's wife understandably tried to flee but the crew of *Cheaters* would not allow her to. (You know how the media are always shoving a mike in someone's face, even if they are lying on a stretcher after being seriously injured.) Four staff members of the show, including host Joel S. Greco, director Hunter Carson, and two security guards allegedly assaulted Maria in their attempt to keep her on camera.

Bobby Goldstein, the creator of *Cheaters*, told the newspaper that the charges were "just nuts" and he joked that he wanted to hire Denny Crane from *Boston Legal* to represent his staff.

Rafael Gutierrez was indicted after this incident for violating an order of protection and has a trial pending for alleged assaults on his wife.

The Long Island Golf Caddie Who Lost to the Female Golfer

Eugene Palumbo, a Long Island golf caddie at the Tallgrass Country Club in Shoreham, New York, lost two golf matches to a female golfer. The club posted and distributed two newsletters making fun of the caddie's manhood. The newsletter, which was distributed by the manager, suggested that the caddie spend his summer vacation in a gay community and provide "lap dances" for the boys. The caddie complained and was fired. The U.S. Equal Employment Opportunity Commission ordered the club to pay the caddie $34,000 for public ridicule. According to the Associated Press, the EEOC said that the incident was sexual harassment, even though the female golfer did not touch the caddie in erotic areas or make lewd comments to him. The lawyer for the club said that the flyers were intended as a joke.

Man Sues Chat-Room Pal

Mike Marlowe and George Gillespie conversed in an
AOL chat room. Marlowe concedes that he teased
Gillespie but says that Gillespie teased him back.
The offended Gillespie did not leave the chat room.
Instead, he did what many Americans do: He sued for
$25,000. His lawsuit claimed that Marlowe and Bob
Charpentier, a fifty-two-year-old resident of Oregon,
insulted and harassed Gillespie in an AOL chat room
called "Romance, Older Men" to the point that it
inflicted "severe emotional distress and physical injury
that is of a nature that no reasonable man could be
expected to endure it." Of course, there is no telling
whether Marlowe and Charpentier have money, so
Gillespie sued AOL for allowing the alleged harassment to take place.

Gillespie charged that Marlowe drove from
Alabama to Ohio and took a picture of Gillespie's
house and posted it on the Internet. Marlowe denied
this. The motivations behind the lawsuit get a bit

weird with regard to Charpentier's role in the harassment. According to Charpentier, he went out on a blind date with a Kentucky woman, a chat room regular, who was also a friend of Gillespie's. After the blind date did not go well, Gillespie insulted Charpentier, calling him a fat, bald, broke old man who sits around in a wheelchair. Charpentier, who has a bad back but does not own a wheelchair, threatened a countersuit. Megan Gray, a Washington, D.C., cyber-issues lawyer, says that AOL can't be held liable for the actions of the members of a chat room and that this was "a loser of a case." Thank God for that.

I Want to Be Readmitted to the Country Club after I Get Out of Jail

Andrew Wiederhorn, the founder of Wilshire Credit Corp. and former CEO of Fog Cutter Capital Group, built a company that repackaged bad loans and securities. It had eight hundred employees and three billion dollars in assets. He lived in a seventeen-thousand-square-foot mansion and traveled in a private jet.

He pleaded guilty to two felonies relating to a financial scandal and spent more than a year in jail. When he got out he returned to his Portland, Oregon, mansion and made his best efforts to be readmitted into the prestigious Multnomah Athletic Club. The club, which was founded in 1891, sprawls over five hundred thousand square feet, and spans two city blocks, refused to let him rejoin.

Wiederhorn filed a lawsuit to get back into the club but a judge dismissed the case because he did not bring his lawsuit within the one-year statute of limitations.

Wiederhorn did not give up, instead perusing the club's twenty-thousand-member list to see what other criminals belong. So far, he has found one arsonist who stole from a locker and people with drug convictions among the members. The club concedes that there are members with criminal records but believes that Mr. Wiederhorn's offenses are worse, particularly since he served jail time.

In a legal filing, the club stated, "If two felony convictions and eighteen months in jail is not sufficient to expel a member from a private club, what is?" Other members have been expelled, including former Oregon governor Neil Goldschmidt, who was kicked out for having a sexual relationship with an underage girl in the 1970s.

Wiederhorn has apparently taken a different viewpoint from classic comedian Groucho Marx, who once quipped, "I would never join a club that would have me as a member."

Don't Make Fun of the Teacher or I Will See You in Court

Alex Davis, a fifteen-year-old Henry County, Georgia, high school student, was sued for defamation by his teacher Robert Muzzillo. According to Muzzillo, he noticed a profile with his name on it posted on MySpace.com. The profile claimed that Muzzillo liked Michael Jackson and was having a "gay old time," like the Fred Flintstone song. According to Davis, he only wrote that Muzzillo lost an eye wrestling with alligators and midgets. Davis said it was just meant as a joke. Even before the lawsuit was filed, the school suspended Davis for three days for his involvement in the incident.

Don't Mess with Lawyers or Reptiles

A Southern California lawyer sued GTE California for listing him under the "Reptiles" heading in its yellow pages. He sought damages in excess of $100,000. The thin-skinned lawyer claims that he suffered ridicule and embarrassment. He became the butt of jokes, received rude phone calls, and dealt with people making hissing sounds at him. It was an honest mistake by GTE. The lawyer's number previously belonged to a business called Reptile Show, and GTE had failed to update its records. As was pointed out by the Web site Gavel2gavel.com, there was some good news for the lawyer: On a positive note, the attorney was listed below "Prehistoric Pets" and "Radical Reptiles." Perhaps he should have been listed under "Sharks."

The Insulting Pharmacist

There are times when an insult is so bad that your gut says someone should pay. The problem is that if you sue, you thereby publicize the insult that hurt you. It is a tad ironic that you spread the harm in order to collect the gelt.

There was such a case down in Palm Beach, Florida, where Janey Karp, a fifty-three-year-old woman who was battling depression and anxiety through prescription medicine, saw something unusual attached to her prescription printout when she went to Walgreen's to pick up her Ambien. In a field reserved for patient information someone had typed "CrAzY!!" and dated it March 17, 2005. In another field, dated September 30, 2004, it read: "She's really a psycho!!! Do not say her name too loud, never mention her meds by names & try to talk to her when . . ." The information continued onto another page that was not attached. Karp claims that when she read this information, she was humiliated and embarrassed. No doubt, as any human being would be.

"I'm thinking they're thinking here comes psycho, that they're laughing at me as I come in the store," she said. "I had enough trouble picking these [medications] up in the first place."

Even taking into account the highly unprofessional nature of the notes, it's clear they were intended as private reminders to the pharmacist. Karp has publicized her case in the newspaper, thereby causing one to wonder how profound her embarrassment really is and whether she, like many before her, is just trying to get paid.

Spielberg Cut Kid's Hair without Permission

The producers of Steven Spielberg's television mini-series *Into the West* were sued by Danny Ponce, a Mescalero Indian, because a set stylist cut his daughter's hair without his permission. With her parents, the daughter had responded to an open casting call near Carrizozo, New Mexico, where the stylist cut her hair to make her look more like an Indian male, because the casting call did not have enough male Indians. "It's part of our culture not to cut a girl's hair until her Coming of Age ceremony," Ponce said. "The only ones allowed to do that are the parents. Nobody asked for permission."

The Mescalero tradition forbids cutting a girl's hair as she approaches puberty. To prepare for womanhood, Mescalero girls participate in a sacred Coming of Age ceremony that requires their hair to reach the waist.

Okay, the hair should not have been cut. As Ponce eloquently put it, "Just because you're wealthy, you don't do something without checking first." So what was the haircut worth to him? How about $250,000 for emotional distress (hurt feelings) and $75,000 in damages.

Dumb-ass Lawsuit

Two California politicians, John Vogel and Paul Grannis, sued Joseph Felice for defamation after Felice listed them on a Web site as numbers one and two on the list of "Top Ten Dumb Asses." The court noted that you cannot sue someone for defamation unless the statement involved can be proved false:

Plaintiffs were justifiably insulted by this epithet, but they failed entirely to show how it could be found to convey a provable factual proposition. If the meaning conveyed cannot by its nature be proved false, it cannot support a libel claim. Judging from additional portions of the Web site offered by plaintiffs in their opposition papers below, the Web site's overall tone was one of puerile vituperation and wretchedly excessive tastelessness. The ostensible author of the list of "Top Ten Dumb Asses," apparently a fictionalized figure, is *himself* presented as a "dumb ass," i.e., "Dumb Ass Bob," who purports to be providing

"advice" to supposed readers who may or may not themselves be fictional or fictionalized. If the page containing the "Top Ten List" is any example, "Dumb Ass Bob" refers to his readers (real or concocted) as "dumb ass[es]." In fact, the main purpose of the page seems to be to employ the term "ass" as often as possible, preferably in conjunction with "dumb." In such a context it is inconceivable that placement on the "Top Ten Dumb Asses" list could be understood to convey any imputation of provable defamatory fact. This statement simply cannot support a defamation claim, or any other claim pleaded by plaintiffs.

And so, there we have it: the dismissal of a dumb-ass lawsuit brought by two dumb-ass politicians.

The Violent Easter Bunny

There is always a built-in defense to any crime: It wasn't me. You are misidentifying me. I am not the criminal. The real guy got away. This would be a difficult defense for Arthur McClure of Fort Myers, Florida, who was dressed up as an Easter bunny and working at a local mall before Easter. His assistant got into an argument with a customer about the early closing of the photo line. McClure, who weighs 280 pounds, joined in. He removed his costume's head and punched the patron in the back of her head. Both McClure and his assistant were arrested. McClure was not photographed for his mug shot in his Easter Bunny outfit, although the arrest report listed his occupation as "Easter Bunny."

Unique Getaway Car

Samuel Dottore, forty-five, of Cleveland, Ohio, stole a frozen roast and needed to get away very quickly. He did not have a car to make the forty-mile trip from the place of the theft, Medina, Ohio, back home to Cleveland. So he decided to steal a golf cart. Dottore broke into the King George Service Company and stole the cart. He took off with the golf cart and even stopped for gas along the way. The police caught him with the cart and the meat. I know this will surprise you: Dottore told the judge that on the day of the crime he had been drinking and the alcohol mixed with his psychiatric medication thereby impairing his judgment. That explains it.

The Nun Bun Caper

Bob Bernstein of Nashville, Tennessee, is the owner of the Bongo Java coffee shop. Bongo Java's Web site proudly describes itself as Nashville's oldest and most celebrated coffeehouse. The café opened Sunday, March 28, 1993, at 4 p.m. and became world famous in December 1996 for the discovery of a cinnamon bun that many believe looks remarkably like Mother Teresa. Bongo Java displayed the bun until 2006, when it was stolen on Christmas morning. Bills and loose change in a charity donation container near the bun's glass display were left untouched.

"What the heck they are going to do with it, I can't imagine," Bernstein said. "It's sure not something any-one would eat. I hope they do eat it. It will teach them a lesson."

The bun was controversial. Bernstein stopped marketing T-shirts and mugs featuring it after Mother Teresa, then eighty-six, wrote him asking him to stop. "She didn't mind the bun itself, but she didn't want us making money off her name or image," said Bernstein. Bernstein also agreed to stop using the words "Mother

Teresa Cinnamon Bun." The coffee shop trade-
marked the two new names Nun Bun and Immaculate
Confection. After some cynical people claimed that the
theft of the Nun Bun was staged as a publicity stunt,
Bernstein offered a five-thousand-dollar reward for
return of the bun, glaze intact and pastry grabber
convicted.

Koranic Fish Disappears

From Kenya comes news of another theft of a religious object, this time a tuna fish that had markings resembling a Koranic text. The fish contained the Arabic inscription "You are the best provider," although no one was certain whether the writing was natural or a hoax. The fish was stolen from the Kenyan Fisheries Department in Mombasa. Someone had offered to buy the fish for $150, although ordinarily it was worth no more than $6. The fisheries department launched a low-profile search for the fish (how do you search for a fish on the low-down?), fearing the anger of Muslims if they heard about the theft.

Garcia's Toilet

A salmon-colored toilet that once belonged to Jerry Garcia, the dead Grateful Dead leader, was stolen from a driveway. A Canadian casino had purchased the toilet for $2,500, intending to use it for marketing. At the time of its theft, the toilet was about to be shipped to the casino, which offered a $250 reward for its return. The police have no suspects and are unclear whether the toilet was stolen by a Deadhead or a thief looking to remodel a bathroom. Deadheads believed that the toilet could have ended up in a rock and roll museum.

Penis Envy

A man went into a McKeesport, Pennsylvania, convenience store and asked the female clerk to warm up the contents of a bag. The clerk put the contents in the microwave but removed it when she smelled an unusual odor. She took a look inside the bag and discovered a severed human penis wrapped in a paper towel. She called the police but the man fled. Police put out an APB for a man lacking a penis.

Then the case got even weirder. A man and woman contacted the police to tell them that the penis was fake and that they had inserted urine in the fake penis that the woman was planning to use to pass a drug test. They had asked the clerk to heat the urine-filled fake penis so that the urine would be body temperature. The couple could face charges of harassment, criminal mischief, and disorderly conduct.

Police chief Joe Pero said, "Hands down the most bizarre . . . I've never come across anything like this before." The McKeesport Police Department has no plans to open a Severed Penis Unit.

The Jury from Hell

A defendant in Memphis, Tennessee, was charged with beating his brother's girlfriend with a brick. He demanded a jury trial and, according to Tennessee defense attorney Leslie Ballin, the court assembled a group of prospective jurors from hell. One left the courtroom after declaring, "I'm on morphine and I'm higher than a kite." After the prosecutor asked the jurors if anyone had been convicted of a crime, a prospective juror volunteered that he had been arrested and taken to a mental hospital after he almost shot his nephew who would not come out from under the bed.

Another prospective juror had alcohol problems and had been arrested for soliciting sex from an undercover officer. "I should have known something was up," the juror said of the sting. "She had all her teeth."

A candid prospective juror stated that he should not be on the jury. "In my neighborhood everyone knows that if you get Ballin [as your lawyer], you are probably guilty." After all was said and done, a jury was picked from this bevy of weird people and in the end, the defendant was found not guilty.

How to Get Out of Jury Duty? First, Don't Try This One

Benjamin Ratliffe of Columbus, Ohio, really did not want to serve on a jury. He filled out a questionnaire for potential jurors and claimed to have "a bad jonesin' for heroin." When asked if he had ever fired a weapon, he wrote, "Yes, I killed someone with it."

Judge Julie M. Lynch held him in contempt and he spent a night in jail. The next day, Ratliffe apologized and charges were dropped. The judge admonished the wise guy, saying, "You do not make a mockery of the process."

Matchmaker, Matchmaker, Make Me a Match...

Anne Majerik paid Orly Hadida, a matchmaker, $125,000 to find her a perfect match. She claims Hadida promised her a cultured gentleman with an estate worth $20 million. Hadida denied this and said that Majerik is a serial litigant who has sued matchmakers in the past. The jurors sided with the plaintiff and awarded her $2 million, although several jurors said they would have awarded up to $20 million—if the money could have gone to charity.

"We wanted to punish the defendant, but . . . we didn't want to reward the plaintiff," said foreman Christie Troutt. "They were both wrong."

It's good to see that there are serious cases being decided each day in the courtrooms of America.

Warning to Corporations: Cigarette Smoking Is Hazardous to Your Financial Health

The surgeon general of the United States determined as early as 1964 that smoking could be hazardous to one's health. A federal statute passed in 1969 required a warning about the dangers of smoking to appear in a conspicuous place on every package of cigarettes sold in the United States. Thirty years later, a class-action lawsuit was filed in Florida on behalf of all of the addicted smokers in the United States. The Florida courts limited the lawsuit to the seven hundred thousand Florida smokers. A two-year jury trial ended in 2000 with the jury determining that the tobacco companies had lied about the dangers of cigarettes, in spite of the warnings. The jury awarded the plaintiffs $145 billion in punitive damages. Obviously, that amount would simply bankrupt the tobacco companies. The Florida court

eventually ruled that the jury couldn't impose punitive damages that are out of proportion to the malice of the act and held that punitive damages should be assessed with regard to an entity's ability to pay.

Why such a case proceeded to trial thirty years after the surgeon general's report is an interesting question. As the *Wall Street Journal* put it, "Personal responsibility and the fact that tobacco companies are selling a legal product are two points that are over-looked by plaintiffs' lawyers and juries more concerned with redistributing corporate wealth."

How to Become a Billionaire

You can become a billionaire by being born into Bill Gates's family, by ingenuity, by being a prince in an Arab oil emirate, or starting to smoke cigarettes at age seventeen and developing lung cancer at age sixty-four. The latter is the life story of Betty Bullock, who sued Philip Morris for fraud and negligence. The jury awarded Bullock $850,000 in compensatory damages and $28 billion in punitive damages. The award thrust Bullock into the billionaire's club. There are only about seven hundred billionaires in the world. Bullock was behind Bill Gates of Microsoft, Warren Buffett of Berkshire Hathaway, and Lawrence Ellison of Oracle. She was ahead of many others, however.

Bad news for Betty: Judge Warren Ettinger thought that the jury's punitive damages award was excessive (wow, he is smart; he may make it to the Supreme Court) and lowered the award to $28 million.

Ordinarily, courts follow the Supreme Court's ruling that "in practice, few awards exceeding a single-digit ratio between punitive and compensatory damages, to a significant degree, will satisfy due process." Not so with

the California Court of Appeals, which upheld the $28 million award, an award thirty-three times the compensatory damages, ruling that Philip Morris's terrible behavior in misleading the public about the health hazards of smoking justified the penalty.

Seattle Police Nab a Killer in a Cold Murder Case

The Seattle police had a tough one on their hands. In 1982, thirteen-year-old Kristen Sumstad was killed. Her body was dumped in a box behind a Seattle store. The police recovered DNA and had a suspect named John Athan.

They did not have a basis or means to get his DNA, so they sent the New Jersey man a phony letter pretending to be lawyers. They said that he was eligible for money in a class-action lawsuit over parking tickets. Athan jumped on the litigation bandwagon and mailed a letter back to them, leaving his saliva on the envelope. The DNA matched DNA recovered from the crime scene and the Seattle police got their man.

Judge Sharon Armstrong said the police deception was legal. The police were allowed to use trickery to catch their prey.

Ohio Foster Mother: "The Children Requested Caged Beds"

Sharon and Michael Gravelle of Wakeman, Ohio, had eleven adopted children. The children, ages one to fourteen, have conditions including autism, fetal alcohol syndrome, and HIV. A three-year-old has a disease called pica, described as an eating disorder in which children compulsively eat items such as dirt or rocks. Police arrested the couple for child endangerment and other charges after discovering that the children slept in cagelike beds with alarms.

Sharon Gravelle testified at a custody hearing that the children had requested the caged beds. She said that as the children got older some of them acted up more, sometimes escaping from their regular beds in the middle of the night to fetch knives from the kitchen or punch each other. She had consulted with Elaie Thompson, an independent social worker, who visited the Gravelle house and approved of the beds.

The husband and wife were both sentenced to two-year jail terms. After sentencing, the couple said they still want their children back. "We still have an inside shot at getting our children back, which was our goal and we still stand by that," said Michael Gravelle. As for Sharon, she lamented how much she missed the little (caged) tikes and said, "I didn't even get a chance to say good-bye" to them.

Crazy (Glue) Love: Part of the Sexual Ritual

Gail O'Toole of Murrysville, Pennsylvania, was convicted of simple assault and put on probation for some bizarre acts she committed against her ex-boyfriend Ken Slaby. O'Toole and Slaby broke up, and then one day O'Toole invited Slaby over to her house. She even picked him up and drove him.

O'Toole was angry about Slaby's new love. Slaby fell asleep at her house and O'Toole glued Slaby's penis to his stomach, his testicle to his leg, and the cheeks of his buttocks together. She also dumped nail polish all over Slaby's head. When Slaby woke up, O'Toole threw him out of her house. Having no car, Slaby walked one mile until he called Murrysville police.

When Officer Joseph Malone showed up, he saw something he had never seen in twenty-three years on the job and quickly took Slaby to the hospital. Rumor has it that doctors thought he was shouting "Oh, tool, Oh, tool." Nurses applied a special oil to dissolve the glue. When it didn't work, they had to peel the glue off

his private parts. Slaby then received treatment from a dermatologist.

Slaby sued O'Toole for damages to his tool and other parts of his body. O'Toole's lawyer thought up a great defense: that the gluing of the penis to his stomach, testicle to his leg, and cheeks of the buttocks together was part of the routine sexual activity between the couple. The jury awarded Slaby $46,000 in damages. The *Pittsburgh Tribune-Review* headline read "Jury Sticks It to Woman."

That Spanking Will Cost You

Janet Orlando, a fifty-three-year-old California woman, sued Alarm One Inc. for $1.7 million for being spanked in front of her coworkers during what Alarm One described as a camaraderie-building exercise. The damages were sought for humiliation. (Apparently there was no injury to the buttocks.) Winners of an Alarm One sales contest poked fun at the losers by throwing pies at them, feeding them baby food, making them wear diapers, and swatting their buttocks with rival companies' sales signs.

"No reasonable middle-aged woman would want to be put up there before a group of young men, turned around to show her buttocks, get spanked and called abusive names, and told it was to increase sales and motivate employees," her lawyer, Nicholas "Butch" Wagner, said in his closing argument.

The defendant's lawyer said the spankings were part of a voluntary program to build camaraderie and were not discriminatory, because they were given to both men and women.

The Fresno, California, jury awarded Orlando $1.7 million: $500,000 for compensatory damages and another $1.2 million in punitive damages.

On one hand, the sales contest was bizarre and offensive. On the other hand, how many of us would agree to be spanked in front of coworkers in exchange for $1.7 million?

In January 2008, a California court reversed the verdict based on a legal error of the trial judge. Orlando's lawyer vowed to retry the case in the hopes that Alarm One will be spanked with a larger verdict than the first one.

Can I Check Your Baggage, Please?

A federal security screener got the surprise of his life when searching the luggage of Myrlene Severe, a Haitian-born permanent U.S. resident, when she was flying home from Haiti. In her luggage was a human skull with organic matter inside. "It still had teeth, hair, and bits of skin and lots of dirt," said Barbara Gonzalez, a spokeswoman for U.S. Immigration and Customs Enforcement in Miami. Apparently, you are not allowed to bring human skulls into the United States.

Severe, who believes in voodoo, had bought the skull from someone in Haiti so she could ward off evil spirits. She was charged with smuggling, failure to declare the head, and transporting hazardous material in air commerce.

Stop Me If You've Heard This One: A Deaf Man and a Legless Man Walk into a Bar...

Kent Hisey, who has two prosthetic legs, and James Mills, who is deaf, met in a New Chicago, Indiana, bar. Hisey agreed to drive Mills home, but got angry with him because Mills had difficulty communicating directions. Hisey got out of the car and used his walker to make his way to the passenger side of the car, where he grabbed Mills and tried to pull him from the car. Mills pushed Hisey to the ground, causing him to hit his head. Police arrested them both. Hisey took a field sobriety test and blew a .16, which is double Indiana's .08 limit. The police had to write Mills a note informing him that he was being arrested for assaulting Hisey.

What Is This Guy Doing Out Here Among Us?

A New Albany, Ohio, father told a fellow theatergoer that Alan Patton, age fifty-four, was looking at his son. The police were called and arrested Patton, a registered sexual predator who had been convicted of rape thirteen years prior. Patton told the police that he would go to the restroom in family restaurants and movie theaters and shut off the water to the child-level urinal and put a cup in the bottom of it. Then he would wait for boys in the bathroom stall. After a child urinated, Patton would go back to the urinal and drink the child's urine.

He claimed to have been addicted to children's urine since he was seven years old. Police believe Patton has been collecting and drinking urine in cities around central Ohio, including Hilliard, Westerville, Dublin, Worthington, and Gahanna.

This case shows the stupidity of the sexual registration program. It is a silly program that protects no one. The better program is a four-letter word: J-A-I-L.

Sir, Please Step Out of the Ladies' Bathroom, Get Up Against the Wall, and Spread Them

When I first started as an assistant district attorney, I would be in arraignments all the time, processing the hundreds of cases that made their way through New York City Criminal Court. The first page of each complaint gave the name of the defendant, his age, and the sex. Why the sex? Well, there were times, particularly in prostitution cases, where one could not be certain.

From New York's Grand Central Terminal comes the story of a phone repairman who underwent sex-change surgery. Apparently, the operation was not that successful because Helena Stone, age seventy, was arrested three times by New York transit police as she tried to use the women's restroom. According to Stone, the officer called her "a freak, a weirdo, and the ugliest

woman in the world" and warned her, "If I ever see you in the women's bathroom, I am going to arrest you."

According to MTA spokesman Tom Kelly, the charges are going to be dropped. After all, this is New York City. Stone's lawyer, Michael Silverman of the Transgender Legal Defense and Education Fund, said he was not aware of the decision to drop the charges against Stone but he welcomed it. Obviously, there is a solution: transgender bathrooms. Stay tuned.

India: That Kiss Will Cost You

Richard Gere played the role of the ugly American on a trip abroad in 2007. His crime: kissing Bollywood star Shilpa Shetty while on a trip to India.

A court issued arrest warrants for both Gere and Shetty, saying that their kiss at a public function "transgressed all limits of vulgarity." Judge Dinesh Gupta of the northwestern city of Jaipur viewed the offending kiss on videotape and called it "highly sexually erotic." The judge found that the two had violated India's strict public obscenity laws, which carry a sentence of three years in jail, a fine, or both. Hindu hardliners in several cities burned effigies of Gere. Meanwhile, Judge Gupta was transferred to a small town in India after he issued the arrest warrant.

Janet Jackson should not offer to do any halftime shows in India.

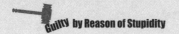

Austria: Holocaust Denier David Irving's Surprise Discovery in Austrian Prison

David Irving, a sixty-seven-year-old British historian, was arrested for Holocaust denial when he entered Austria. Irving had given lectures denying the existence of the gas chambers. Under Austrian law, Holocaust denial is a criminal offense punishable by up to twenty years in jail.

As Irving awaited trial, he was incarcerated in Graz prison. He visited the library and found two of his own books there, *Hitler's War* and *The Destruction of Convoy PQ.17*, which had been translated into German. Irving autographed them for prison guards. A red-faced prison warden did not know how the books got into the library. *Hitler's War* was the first volume of Irving's two-part biography of Hitler and sought to describe the war from the dictator's point of view.

The only thing that would have topped this would be if Irving were told by the prison librarian that *Mein Kampf* was on loan to another prison and would be available shortly.

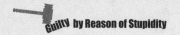

David Irving pleaded guilty to criminal charges and received a three-year jail sentence, although he claimed at sentencing that he was mistaken when he said that the idea that there were gas chambers at Auschwitz was a fairy tale.

Mexico: South-of-the-Border Silliness

In the midst of the debate over immigration reform in the United States, President Bush proposed using the National Guard to patrol the southern border and prevent illegal entry. Mexico leaped into action, saying that it would file lawsuits in the United States if National Guard troops became involved in detaining illegal aliens. That would be an interesting lawsuit. The grounds would be what? "You Americans have no right to prevent our citizens from illegally entering your country"?

In other news, Angel Maturino Resendiz killed at least fifteen people near railroad tracks in the United States. On June 27, 2006, the Mexican drifter was executed in Texas for the slaying of Dr. Claudia Benton

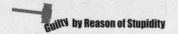

seven and a half years prior. Resendiz had slipped across the U.S. border and roamed around the country in freight trains. DNA evidence linked him to the murder.

The consular general of Mexico appealed to the court to prevent the execution, challenging the defendant's competency and saying that lethal injection was a cruel and inhumane punishment.

If you take these two stories together, it adds up to this: Mexico believes that Mexicans have an absolute right to come into the United States without permission and if they kill, Texas and other states have no right to punish them in the same manner applied to U.S. murderers. Makes sense, right?

Italy: Rape Is Okay If the Victim Is Not a Virgin

Marco T. of Sardinia was convicted of sexual violence and threats against the fourteen-year-old daughter of his live-in girlfriend and sentenced to more than three years in prison. For comparison, under New York law, the sentence for such a rape would range from six to twenty-five years.

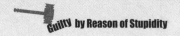

The Italian Supreme Court reduced Marco's sentence to three years because "since the age of thirteen [the girl] had had many sexual relations with men of every age. And it's right to assume that at the time of the encounter with the suspect, her personality, from a sexual point of view, was much more developed than what one might normally expect from a girl of her age."

Using logic like that, one would assume that the court would treat the rape of a seventy-year-old grandmother with leniency since such a grandmother, having had sexual relations over several decades, would not suffer trauma from a rape.

The decision provoked an outcry around Italy and was condemned by UNICEF.

Italy: If You Believe Jesus Existed, You Are Going to Pay

Lifelong atheist Luigi Cascioli, age seventy-two, sued Rev. Enrico Righi, a seventy-five-year-old parish priest, for claiming that Jesus Christ existed. Cascioli filed a civil suit under an Italian law prohibiting deceptive

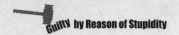

advertising. Righi wrote in a church newsletter that Jesus was born in Bethlehem to a couple named Mary and Joseph and that he lived in Nazareth. Cascioli claimed that was an "abuse of popular belief." According to Cascioli, Righi's parish has profited financially from promoting "the fable of Christ's life" and the church is guilty of impersonation by confusing the persona of Jesus with another man named John of Gamala, said to have lived in Israel around the time of Jesus. Cascioli has the burden of proof in this action.

Meanwhile, Rev. Righi has not caved in to the pressure of the lawsuit. He said, "Cascioli says that Christ never existed. If he doesn't see the sun at midday, he shouldn't denounce me just because I do see it."

The case is starting to sound like *Miracle on 34th Street* or *Oh, God!* with George Burns.

Meanwhile in New York City, Judge Diane Lebedeff granted the application of Jose Luis Espinal, age forty-two, to change his name to Jesus Christ. Why did he do it? Because a year prior it dawned on him that "I am the person that is that name. You're dealing with the real deal."

Lebedeff cited precedent from a 2001 Utah case

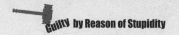

in which a man was permitted to change his name to Santa Claus.

Perhaps Rev. Righi should call Jose Luis Espinal, I mean Jesus Christ, as a witness at the upcoming trial in Italy.

Japan: A Burglar with a Nice Touch

Lee Jin-Se broke into an apartment in Tokyo and stole 210,000 yen (about $2,100) and the thirty-five-year-old victim's cash card. He also tied her up. But after tying her up, he showed the world that he is capable of rehabilitation by giving her a shoulder massage for several hours. After he was arrested, Lee Jin-Se told police that he gave her the massage "to relax her."

If burglars around the world would follow this example, burglaries would be a lot less stressful.

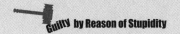

Scotland: Don't Beat the Dog That Guides You

A blind Scotsman was quite angry at his guide dog, because the dog refused to cross a busy street. The blind man bit the dog's head and then kicked the Labrador retriever mix. An eyewitness to this vicious attack reported it to the Edinburgh police. David Todd, age thirty-four, was arrested and charged with cruelty to animals and breach of the peace.

Turkey: Sticks and Stones May Break My Bones ...

Article 301 of Turkey's penal code makes it a crime to insult Turkey, Turkishness, or the government, and is an obstacle to the country joining the European Union. Recep Tayyip Erdogan, Turkey's prime minister, regularly files lawsuits over personal insults and won $3,400 in a case against a journalist who suggested the prime minister might be mentally ill. Most recently, Elif Shafak, one of Turkey's leading authors, was

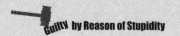

acquitted of Article 301 charges in a case involving a work of fiction that allegedly insulted Turkishness. Prime Minister Erdogan says, "Criticism is one thing, insulting is another."

Australia: Cadaver Abuse in the Land Down Under

Four staff members of an Australian university are being investigated for mistreating cadavers by fondling breasts and vaginas and using a head for degrading purposes (whatever that means). Some whistle-blowers came forward to report this abuse. Professor Fred Hilmer said the identities of staff whistle-blowers would be safeguarded under the Protected Disclosures Act.

Japan: Lazy Car Thief's Road to Prison

A Japanese man saw an empty police car with its engine running beside a post office and hopped in and drove home with it. "I came out shopping by train, but I got tired of walking, so I thought I would drive the police car home," the man told cops. The cops arrested the lazy car thief about fifteen minutes later in the driveway of his home, approximately two and a half miles away.

Sweden: Smoker Sued for Smoking in Her Own Garden

A Swedish woman was sued for smoking in her own garden by her next-door neighbor, who said he was

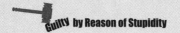

hit with cigarette smoke every time he left the house and was unable to open his windows. The lawsuit demanded $2,999 along with a $280 fine each time she lights up in the future.

The neighbor, of course, is a lawyer. How did you guess? The defendant, a forty-nine-year-old single mom, complained, "It makes me sad and angry. Should somebody else be able to control my life?"

China: Chinese Make Mountain Out of Molehill

Weng Zhendong was the chairman of a Chinese company that promised investors up to 60 percent returns for buying kits of ants and breeding equipment from two companies he set up. Ants are used in some traditional Chinese medicinal remedies. More than ten thousand people invested before investigators shut down his companies. One investor who was swindled committed suicide. Of the $385 million Weng cheated out of investors, only $1.28 million was recovered. China sentenced him to death for his fraud.

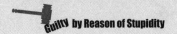

Saudi Arabia:
Party Time in Saudi Arabia Has Its Risks

Religious police busted a party in Jidda and arrested 433 foreigners, including some 240 women. The prosecutor charged them with "drinking, arranging for an impudent party, mixed dancing, and shooting a video for the party." Judge Saud al-Boushi sentenced twenty of the partygoers, all of whom were foreign, to prison terms of three to four months and ordered them to receive an unspecified number of lashes.

Marriage Contract of Wifely Expectations

Travis Frey, a thirty-three-year-old man from Iowa, was arrested for trying to kidnap his own wife. After his arrest, his wife provided the police with a four-page "Contract of Wifely Expectations." This contract, which his wife did not sign, set out the terms of hygiene, clothing, and sexual activities Frey expected. If the wife had a good day, she received a GBD (good behavior day), allowing her to get out of doing things. Among the rules:

Hygiene and Self Care: You will shave every third day, which includes underarms, chest, legs, and pubic area (navel to anus). All areas are to be completely clean shaven.

Clothing and Other Apparel: You will wear only thigh-high garters and only thong panties. The only exception would be during your menstrual cycle. You will give me all non-thong panties, all

tights, all knee-high, and/or ankle-high nylons. You may keep five pairs of non-thong panties of your choice for use during the menstrual cycle.

My Time: When we are at home and alone as a family, from when you are naked until midnight, will be My Time. This time will be time you devout [*sic*] to me, whereas you will be in my service to do *anything and everything* I want, which may or may not be sexual in manner.

Sex Slave Contract

Travis Frey is not the only psycho with marriage contracts of wifely expectations. Kevin Anderson, a Wisconsin businessman, concocted his own six-page contract for his wife, Kimberly O'Brien. The contract, which indicates "it is not binding in a court of law" (that falls under the category of "No s–t, Sherlock"), outlines the punishment that O'Brien would receive if she failed to abide by its terms. In the introductory paragraph, Kevin is referred to as "Master" and Kimberly as "Slave." The contract, ignorant of the Thirteenth Amendment, which freed the slaves, is referred to as a 100 Percent Slavery Contract. Among the clauses:

- Slave agrees at all times to make her body readily available to Master for use. Slave agrees to wear any and all clothing Master chooses.
- Slave shall address Master as "Master Jon" at all times without fail. Slave shall pay full attention to Master when spoken to. The slave shall sit, stand, walk, kneel, and lay where, when, and how Master

desires. Slave shall not remove any restraint device for any other reason other than an emergency.

- Training activities include daily discipline and instructions, proper answers, bondage, and self-bondage.

    Discipline includes bondage and restraint, leash training, implements of discipline, and body and foot worship.

- Mild punishments are nipple pinching and time-outs. Medium punishments entail genital pinching and intense bondage time. Severe punishments include panty or ball gags and caning.

Both Frey in a criminal case and Anderson in a divorce lawsuit have memorialized their sick-pup minds in writing. This will not be lost on the jury.

If You Commit Suicide, You Can Get Arrested and Go Straight to Jail

In certain jurisdictions it is a crime to commit suicide. Yes, the law punishes those who attempt suicide by prosecution, conviction, and jail sentences. (Logically, the law only applies to those who unsuccessfully attempt suicide, since if you succeed, you obviously cannot be prosecuted.)

One woman chose the wrong time to commit suicide: She hanged herself from a fifteen-foot branch on October 27 around 9 p.m. Motorists in Frederica, Delaware, noticed her hanging from the tree the next day around 7:30 a.m. but the authorities were not called until 10:55 a.m. The explanation was not apathy, indifference, or callousness of local residents: Passersby thought the suicide victim was a Halloween display.

Apparently, this is not an isolated incident. On a leafy block in New York City's Greenwich Village, a man dressed entirely in black leather, including a

head mask, was found hanging from a fence right by a delicatessen. The deli owner, Intravadan Patel, forty-six, saw the leather-clad body early in the morning but did not call the police because he mistook it for a Halloween decoration.

"I thought it was one of those scary dummies; a woman came in, said it was a human being [and told me to] call the police." The body was discovered on September 27, 2006, a full month before Halloween. This was not lost on Patel, who said, "I was wondering why they put up the decorations early."

The man might have been choked to death by a dog collar, which was around his neck; the other end of the dog collar was strapped around the three-foot-tall fence post. Authorities were unclear whether the death was a result of suicide or a bizarre autoerotic sex game.

Surgeon General's Warning: Hibachi Chefs Can Be Dangerous to Your Health

The estate of Jerry Colaitis sued Benihana, a Japanese steakhouse chain, for $10 million, claiming Colaitis had wrenched his neck when he ducked to avoid a shrimp the hibachi chef had tossed at him. Colaitis's attorney claimed that Colaitis died from complications resulting from the neck surgery he required after the incident.

The Benihana chefs grill food in front of customers and entertain them as they cook. They often toss food to customers to see if they can catch it. During the trial, chefs testified that the food tossing "had become common" after the release of a Jackie Chan movie in the 1990s.

According to Colaitis's attorney, the hibachi chef struck Colaitis's brother-in-law in the forehead with a shrimp and then burned his son's arm with a second shrimp toss. Colaitis jerked his neck away to avoid being hit by the third sizzling shrimp.

Colaitis ate at Benihana in January 2001, and went in for neck surgery in June 2001. The cause of death was sepsis, a severe infection. The defense claimed that the infection was unrelated to the shrimp toss.

Colaitis's attorney argued to the jury that Benihana chief chef Toro Hasegawa testified that he agreed it was dangerous for chefs to toss food. The jury tossed the case in two hours, finding for the defendant.

"Quick, Emergency, I Need a Cutie-Pie Deputy with a Nightstick"

The neighbors of Lorna Jeanne Dudash of Aloha, Oregon, called the sheriff's office to complain about noise coming from her home. When the deputy showed up, Dudash liked what she saw.

After the deputy left, she called 911 and asked that the "cutie-pie deputy" return. Dudash told the operator, "He's the cutest cop I've seen in a long time. I just want to know his name. Heck, it doesn't come very often a good man comes to your doorstep."

The dispatcher asked Dudash why the deputy should return. Dudash told the incredulous dispatcher, "Honey, I'm just going to be honest with you, OK? I just thought he was cute. I'm forty-five years old and I'd just like to meet him again, but I don't know how to go about doing that without calling 911," she said.

"I know this is absolutely not in any way, shape, or form an emergency, but if you would give the officer

by Reason of Stupidity

my phone number and ask him to come back, would you mind?"

The deputy did return and once he verified that there was no emergency (lonely heart notwithstanding), he arrested Dudash for misusing the 911 system.

No Good Deed Goes Unpunished

Mark Morice commandeered the boat of John Lyons during the flooding that followed Hurricane Katrina. According to Morice, he saved more than two hundred people, including Irving Gordon, a ninety-three-year-old dialysis patient Morice carried from his home to the boat.

"I don't know where we would be today if it weren't for him," said Molly Gordon, Irving Gordon's wife of sixty-five years.

According to Morice, he left Lyons's boat for other rescuers to use. Under the circumstances, returning the boat was "the farthest thing from my mind." But John Lyons never got his boat back.

John Lyons sued Morice for taking his boat without permission and not returning it. Lyons's lawyer, E. Ronald Mills, contended that Lyons suffered "grief, mental anguish, embarrassment, and suffering . . . due to the removal of the boat," as well as the cost of the boat itself.

Morice's lawyer displayed photographs and videos that Morice took depicting desperate high-water scenes and the screams and poundings of people apparently trapped inside their attics.

Lyons learned that Morice had taken his boat when Morice called Lyons's wife to tell her why he did so. He also e-mailed the Lyonses a picture that showed how he saved people with the boat.

When Lyons got only half the replacement value of the boat from his insurance company, he sent Morice a letter asking for twelve thousand dollars to "settle the matter." E. Ronald Mills criticized Morice, saying he could have been more responsible when he took the boat: "If I felt I had to take the boat, I would have at least left a note," Mills said.

Morice replied, "Next time there's a major storm or natural disaster and I'm called to save lives, I'll try to remember to bring a pen and paper."

The media frenzy surrounding Lyons's lawsuit was too much for him to bear. Five days after filing the lawsuit, Lyons's lawyer dismissed it. Mr. Morice, the Good Samaritan, was delighted by Mr. Lyons's change of heart.

The Court Says No Need for Politically Correct Driver's License

Sultaana Freeman, an American-born Muslim woman, was not issued a Florida driver's license after she refused to remove her hijab (veil or head scarf) for the photo. She sued the state of Florida for violating a statute that prohibits the government to "substantially burden a person's exercise of religion."

Florida authorities argued that the world changed after 9/11. Thirteen of the nineteen 9/11 hijackers allegedly obtained licenses in Florida. In response to this, Florida authorities cracked down on the system, noting that DMV photos are one reliable way to identify a person.

Freeman said that it was her "sincere religious belief that her religion requires her to wear her veil in front of strangers and unrelated males." Freeman believes that photographs of the human face and animals are prohibited and does not allow photographs of faces in her home. Freeman's daughter plays with faceless dolls, and if Freeman buys something from a grocery store that has a face on it, she covers it with Wite-Out.

According to Florida DMV, when Muslim women are photographed, all men leave the room, the woman lifts her veil, her picture is taken, she puts the license in her pocketbook, and nobody sees it again. That is, of course, unless she gets pulled over by the police.

A nonjury trial was conducted before Florida circuit court judge Janet Thorpe. Judge Thorpe rejected Freeman's request to wear the veil during the DMV photo, finding that it did not substantially burden her right to practice her religion. The state had a compelling interest in maintaining a photo image identification since such a system was essential to promote the state's interest in protecting the public.

The ACLU appealed Judge Thorpe's decision to the district court of appeals. The court noted that in Freeman's deposition she had testified that she must be veiled in the presence of men not related to her. This meant that her religious beliefs did not prevent her from being photographed at all. The state of Florida

accommodated Freeman by having a female photographer photograph her. The Florida court quoted the U.S. Supreme Court in stating "(W)e are a cosmopolitan nation made up of people of almost every conceivable religious preference. . . . Consequently, it cannot be expected, much less required, that legislators enact no law regulating conduct that may in some way result in . . . disadvantage to some religious sects."

As reported by the Associated Press, Freeman was photographed without a veil after she was arrested in 1998 on a domestic battery charge.

A Jack-of-All-Delivery-Guys: Domino's and the Dead

A Lower Southampton Township, Pennsylvania, police officer pulled over a 1993 Buick after noticing that the car did not have an inspection sticker. The driver, William Bethel, twenty-four, was driving with a suspended license, and the cops told him the vehicle was going to be impounded. That's when things got a little bit interesting.

The station wagon that Bethel was driving had a stretcher in the back of it, along with rubbish, wet clothing, and pizzas. Bethel told the cops that after he finished delivering Domino's pizzas, he used the station wagon to transport deceased bodies for a funeral home. The police checked with local health officials and determined that Bethel had violated no local health ordinances. The station wagon was registered to a body-removal service that delivers to Philadelphia-area funeral homes.

Why is it not against the law to deliver the deceased along with Domino's pizzas? Probably because no one had thought that anyone would be bizarre enough to do this.

Search for Tiger in Manhattan Apartment Building Is Legal: What a Shock!

Antoine Yates lived on the fifth floor of a Harlem apartment building. It is tough to have pets in New York, but Yates managed to live there with his pet Ming, a ten-foot long, 450-pound tiger, and a six-foot alligator named Al.

Ming bit off a chunk of Yates's leg, and Yates lied to the police about it, telling them he had been bitten by a large brown-and-white pit bull. Two days later, an anonymous caller told the police that Yates was living in his apartment with a tiger. An NYPD officer rappelling off the side of the building managed to shoot Ming with a tranquilizer dart. Ming ran through the apartment and collapsed after fifteen minutes and was taken to an animal refuge. Yates was convicted of reckless endangerment and spent three and a half months in jail.

When he got out, he sued the cops for an illegal search of his apartment, claiming the police stole cash and jewelry while sedating the tiger. Federal judge Sidney Stein dismissed the lawsuit, noting that the police could not enter the apartment because there was a tiger in the apartment that had recently mauled a man. The police acted reasonably, Judge Stein noted, since the law forbids harboring illegal pets like tigers.

Yates told the police that he bought the tiger from a woman in Minnesota and had owned monkeys and scorpions before owning Ming.

Judge Stein conceded that judges overuse the word *chutzpah*, Yiddish for "audacity," but in this particular case it was the "most appropriate term to use" in referring to Yates's lawsuit.

Dead Men Don't Take Vioxx

Cheryl Rogers sued Merck in Alabama, claiming that her husband, Howard, had died of a heart attack after taking Vioxx. Merck asked Rogers to provide evidence in the form of the written prescription showing that Howard actually had taken Vioxx. Rogers claimed he had taken a sample given to him by his family doctor. She provided the remaining Vioxx pills in the sample packs. Rogers insisted that she was standing next to her husband when he was given three sample packs of Vioxx.

Merck checked the samples, and their lot numbers showed that those particular pills did not arrive at Merck's distribution warehouse until six months after Rogers had died. Judge John Rochester, who presided over the case, refused to dismiss it and ordered a settlement conference.

Interestingly, Judge Rochester had received sixty thousand dollars in campaign contributions in 2004 from political action committees funded by the law firm that filed the suit against Merck. These contributions went to Judge Rochester's unsuccessful campaign for a seat on the Alabama Supreme Court.

Wake Up and Smell the Options

Do dead men have options? Yes, according to cable TV operator Cablevision, which granted stock options to company vice chairman Mark Lustgarten after he died. The company improperly backdated the options, permitting Lustgarten's estate to exercise approximately four hundred thousand of them. Because of options given to Lustgarten and four other employees, Cablevision overstated profits by $89 million over ten years.

Vioxx Juror Gets Dough from Plaintiff

Leonel Garza, a seventy-one-year-old overweight smoker who took Vioxx for three weeks, died in Texas of a heart attack. Garza's widow, Felicia Garza, brought a lawsuit in the small town of Rio Grande City, Texas. Merck had tried to move the trial to federal court since corporations consider Rio Grande City a pro-plaintiff jurisdiction.

During jury selection, one prospective juror, Jose Rios, told the court that he knew Felicia Garza because he worked as a custodian at the school where she worked as a teacher. Given the fact that this was a small town, this was not unusual and Rios was chosen to serve on the jury.

Garza had high cholesterol, a history of a heart attack, and had had a quadruple bypass, yet the jury awarded his survivors $7 million, plus punitive damages. The total judgment against Merck was $32 million.

After the trial a fifty-year-old school administrator, Oneida Saenz, alerted Merck's lawyers to the fact that Garza had lent Rios money. Saenz had known both

Garza and Rios for years and had actually witnessed the two exchange money, which Saenz says Garza stored "in her bosom."

Merck lawyers learned that Jose Rios had borrowed thousands of dollars over the years from Felicia Garza. Rios did not disclose to the court that he had borrowed $2,500 from Garza in June 2005 and had paid her back at the end of that year. Two months later, he served on Garza's jury.

With this new information, Merck got permission to depose Jose Rios. Subpoenaed cell phone records revealed that Rios called Garza's cell phone the night before jury selection, after he was summoned as a juror. There were also four phone calls from Rios to Garza the day that Merck filed its motion to depose him.

Garza's lawyers say that Rios had honestly answered the questions put to him during the jury selection process, and since he was not asked about loans, he did not have to volunteer any information.

But Oneida Saenz aptly put it, when explaining why she came forward, "I just want to be fair. Do it the right way—not having your compadre or your friend be part of the jury."

Of All the Gin Joints in All the Towns...

There are times when police feel fortunate that criminals are so stupid. Westlake, Ohio, police must have been grateful to this mentally challenged defendant.

The wallet of a waitress at a Lakewood bar was stolen on July 9. Her driver's license and credit card were inside. On July 25, Maria Berga walked into Moosewood Saloon and ordered a drink. When she was asked to show identification, she showed the waitress a copy of her own license. The waitress called the police and Berga fled the saloon.

When Berga was arrested, she told the police that she was given the license by a friend of a friend. She did not explain why she was using the license, since she was of drinking age, nor did she indicate whether she realized that the woman on the license picture was her waitress.

The credit card had $1,000 of unauthorized purchases and police tried to determine if they could connect the charges to Berga. Perhaps she even signed her own name to these charges. Who knows? In a case like this, even that is possible.

Order in the Court!
I'll Have Scotch on the Rocks

Joshua Baury, a twenty-five-year-old Pennsylvania resident, was arrested for DUI with a blood-alcohol level of .17. The legal limit was .08.

Baury really knew how to get the judge on his side. He showed up to his court appearance drunk. In courtroom testimony, Baury told the judge that he drinks twelve beers a day "and then some" and that he was on medication for a bipolar disorder. Baury's blood-alcohol level on the day he was in court was .20. Carbon County president judge Roger Nanovic gave Baury a thirty-day sentence for showing up drunk and a similar sentence for his DUI charges that resulted in a car crash.

Now there is a man who knows how to win friends and influence judges.

"Thank You, Jesus" Can Get You a Jail Sentence

Junior Stowers was arrested and charged with hitting his fifteen-year-old son with a broomstick. The son eventually recanted his accusation and claimed that he injured himself when his brother hit him with a car door.

Just before the jury reached a verdict, Hawaii circuit court judge Patrick Border called both lawyers to the bench and warned them that neither side was to show emotion at the reading of the verdict. Stowers, the defendant, was never told anything by his lawyer, and when the jury announced a verdict of "not guilty," Stowers raised his hands and said, "Thank you, Jesus."

Judge Borders held Stowers in contempt for what he characterized as an "outburst" and the defendant, who would have otherwise been free to leave the courtroom, spent six hours in a cell.

Judge Border had found Stowers's "nonverbal gestures and outbursts to be disruptive and improper, regardless of content."

Stowers's lawyer, Susan Arnett, noting that Stowers is a devoutly religious man, indicated that Stowers's pastor and family members were upset that someone could land in jail for thanking Jesus.

Poor Judge Border needed an escape hatch out. This was going to become a media nightmare. He dropped the charges, noting that defense attorney Arnett did not have time to tell Stowers about the court's order not to show emotion when the verdict was announced.

One Man's Terrorist Is Another Man's Freedom Fighter

Four thousand foreign citizens, mostly Israeli, filed a class-action suit against Arab Bank, a Jordanian bank with a New York branch, in federal district court in Brooklyn. The plaintiffs claimed that Arab Bank had used offices in the West Bank and Gaza to pay the families of suicide bombers who had attacked them or their relatives during the Intifada.

Among the attacks that formed the basis of the plaintiff's claims were suicide bombings that killed civilians in restaurants, malls, seaside pubs, and dance clubs. According to the plaintiff, most of the money dispensed to the terrorists' families by Arab Bank came from Saudi Arabian "charities." The *New York Post* reported that terror groups such as Hamas provided "martyr kits" to the families of suicide bombers. After filing out the forms in these kits, the suicide bomber's family presented the kit to the Arab Bank and received

payment of $5,316.06 for each suicide bomber. The Arab Bank helped administer the program, determining the eligibility of each suicide bomber's family and dispensing the funds.

The plaintiffs brought the lawsuit under the Alien Tort statute, which allows foreign citizens to bring lawsuits arising from human-rights violations anywhere in the world to America's federal courts. The U.S. Supreme Court recently ruled that only the most egregious human-rights violations qualify, such as genocide and slavery. The Supreme Court spoke of a violation of norms that have been accepted by "civilized nations."

Enter Kevin Walsh, a partner with a well-known corporate firm called Leboeuf, Lamb, Greene, and MacRae. Walsh demonstrates that when it comes to making arguments to try to win for your client, anything goes.

Walsh argued that the federal court could not hear the plaintiffs' case since terrorism against Israel does not violate any "international norm." Eighty Islamic and African nations do not consider Arab suicide bombers to be terrorists, since the conduct of those

terrorists furthers the rights of self-determination of a people. Of course Walsh and bank lawyers did not address the fact of whether the nations in question constitute "civilized nations" and whether those same nations would consider the attack on the World Trade Center to be justifiable as an act of self-defense against America, the Great Satan.

Walsh said that since there is no uniform consensus as to the Palestinian-Israeli conflict, the plaintiffs could not sue because suicide bombings are not universally held to be violations of the norms of civilized nations.

The plaintiffs' lawyer, Gregory Joseph, argued that the failure of some countries to condemn Palestinian suicide bombers was irrelevant to the plaintiffs' right to sue. "We have a bank in New York paying bounties on the bodies of dead civilians. It would be a remarkable ruling for the court to conclude that the widespread and systematic killing of civilians was not a violation of international law."

Walsh, arguing to federal district court judge Nina Gershon that the case should be dismissed, quoted from a federal court decision that states, "Nor have we shaken ourselves free of the cliché that 'one man's terrorist is another man's freedom fighter.'"

Interestingly, Lebouf, Lamb has a Riyadh, Saudi Arabia, office and represents many Saudi Arabian corporations.

Judge Nina Gershon denied Arab Bank's motion to dismiss the lawsuit. She wrote, "Arab Bank provided financial assistance to the organizations sponsoring the suicide bombings and helped them further their goal of encouraging bombers to serve as 'martyrs.'"

Low-Profile Arrest

If you want to avoid arrest, you should try to maintain a low profile. Ask Joe Cullen, Detroit Lions defensive line coach, who managed to get arrested two times in one week. On August 24, 2006, Coach Cullen was arrested in Dearborn, Michigan, for driving naked. The police ticket read "driving on a public street without any clothes on (NUDE)."

As if that was not bad enough, on September 1, 2006, Cullen was arrested again in Dearborn, this time for drunk driving. Cullen's blood-alcohol level of .12 was above the legal limit of .08. The good news was that Cullen was wearing clothes at the time of the second arrest.

Cullen issued a statement through the team: "I would like to apologize to the Detroit Lions organization, our fans, my family, and friends for any embarrassment these incidents have caused. These incidents represent a mistake in judgment on my part. I deeply regret them and have learned a valuable lesson. It won't happen again."

Ah, yes, a mistake in judgment. As Cullen was about to get into his car, he debated whether to put on clothes or to drive naked. He considered both options and made a mistake in judgment by deciding to drive without clothes. And then there was that valuable lesson: You have to get dressed before driving in public.

It must have been interesting to handcuff and fingerprint a naked man. No frisk was necessary. The police did not release the mug-shot photo.

Lions president Matt Millen acknowledged that "these are very serious matters," and said, "Cullen requested immediate help in seeking treatment. . . . A comprehensive, private program has been established for him."

Perhaps his psychiatrist will place a sign on Cullen's dashboard: "Put on your pants before starting the vehicle."

Baby Shower Gone Bad

A twenty-two-year-old mother-to-be had a baby shower in Springfield, Massachusetts, that she will never forget. It erupted into a fight over a very important issue: Should a woman at the party let her five-year-old drink beer? When the mother-to-be tried to intervene, one of the attendees, Jazz Rivas, began hitting her with a large stick. Partygoer Juan Velazquez fired his gun into the crowd, striking Aristotle Garcia, who had been fighting with another guest, in the stomach.

Juan Velazquez was arrested and charged with assault and battery with a deadly weapon and armed assault with intent to murder. Antonio Santiago, the man Aristotle Garcia was fighting with, was similarly charged. Jazz Rivas was charged with assault and battery on a pregnant female and other charges.

For some people, you can't go to a baby shower without bringing your piece. Once you get there, if things get out of hand, "all's fair in love and war"; even the pregnant guest of honor is fair game.

"Doctor, Can You Give Me a Hand?"

Ahmed Rashed, age twenty-six, a 2005 graduate of the University of Medicine and Dentistry of New Jersey in Newark, was arrested and charged with stealing a hand from a cadaver scheduled for cremation and giving it to Linda Kay, an exotic dancer. The doctor, who was a medical student at the time he gave the stripper a hand, had met Kay at a club, and—although it is unclear how this came up in the conversation—she asked him for a cadaver's hand. When a stripper makes a request, you comply.

Kay kept the hand in a jar of formaldehyde in her bedroom. Authorities found it in her dresser. She had affectionately named the hand "Freddy." ("Thing" was already taken.) The police discovered the hand, along with six human skulls, when they went to Kay's home to investigate a call of a suicidal roommate. According to Kay's mother, Kay had ordered the skulls from a mail-order catalog.

Donald A. DiGioia, Kay's lawyer, explained the media's interest in the case: "Obviously the case has taken on a level of interest because of her background and occupation. All I can say is that different people have different interests."

During the court proceeding, Rashed apologized, telling the court he meant no harm and had outgrown the immaturity he displayed. His lawyer, Kalman Geist, said he made a silly mistake. He pleaded guilty to third-degree theft, was fined $5,000, and ordered to stay out of trouble for fifteen months—a relative "slap on the wrist." The Maimonides Medical Center in New York was the beneficiary of Rashed's unique medical skills. He became a resident there and was still eligible to apply for a license to practice medicine in New Jersey.

The judge deserves a hand for that brilliant sentence.

Life Imitates Art:
Gitmo Terrorist's Pet Ant

In Woody Allen's album *Standup Comic*, he tells of how poor he was when growing up. He says that his family could not afford a dog. Instead, he was given a pet ant. Once someone was bullying him and he urged Spot, his pet ant, to attack the bully. The bully stepped on his pet.

Now comes Zachary Katznelson, a lawyer, who brings a lawsuit against the U.S. government in which he alleges that his client, Shaker Aamer, has been kept in solitary confinement at the prison in Guantanamo Bay.

"His only consistent contact with living beings beside his captors is with the ants in his cell. He feeds them and considers them his friends," Katznelson told the court. Katznelson also alleged that his client was choked, his nose was bent, and his eyes gouged. Army captain Dan Byer, a Gitmo spokesman, denied the charges.

Aamer had another complaint that he passed on to his lawyer Katznelson: The air conditioner is often turned off, leaving him sweating profusely in the

tropical heat, or turned up full blast "so the cell is freezing cold." It is interesting that an air-conditioning problem—usually a minor husband-wife debate—is the subject of a federal lawsuit.

Aamer claimed that he was working for a charitable organization in Afghanistan when he was captured after 9/11. A former resident of Britain, Maryland, and Georgia, Aamer has been accused by the United States of once sharing an apartment with convicted terror plotter Zacarias Moussaoui and receiving money directly from Osama bin Laden.

Katznelson concedes, "There is no question in my mind that [Aamer] is mentally unstable." Yet, it is this mentally unstable client whose word Katznelson trusts in claiming that his nose was bent and his eyes gouged.

In the war against Islamofascists, our citizens and allies are beheaded; our enemies—the prisoners at Gitmo—are not given adequate air-conditioning and can only speak to pet ants.

Don't Let the Bedbugs Bite

A couple sued the Nevele Hotel in New York's Catskill Mountains, alleging they had suffered bedbug bites when they stayed there in the summer of 2005. Leslie Fox endured five hundred bedbug bites and had to be treated with steroids. Fox went on *Good Morning America* and told the morning audience, "To this day I am left with evidence of the bites in the form of pigmentation scars all over my body."

Pictures of the nasty bites on Fox's back appeared on the Internet. The bites were not the only reason Fox and her husband filed a $20 million lawsuit (that works out to $40,000 per bite). There was also the resulting psychological damage done to Fox. According to Fox, she now travels with a flashlight and magnifying glass to help search for bedbugs.

"I could not spend a night in a strange bed without thoroughly inspecting it," she said. "Every sensation on my skin, I would wonder if something wasn't lurking in the room, under the bed, and attacking me again." The *Wall Street Journal*'s headline read, "The Catskills: Known for Dirty Dancing; Accused of Dirty Bedding."

Okay, so you think that the lawsuit has merit, even if $40,000 per bite is excessive. The punch line will get you: Joseph O'Connor, a lawyer for the hotel, noted the following minor detail about the Foxes and their bug-bite lawsuit:

I'd like to see the bedbug that caused the $20 million injury to this person. This very guest booked a room immediately after the bedbug incident, and was there two weeks later and stayed for approximately five days without complaint or harm, so I think it's a little disingenuous to allege they were damaged to the amount of $20 million and continue to have psychological damage as a result of staying the first time at the Nevele.

And what was Leslie Fox's response to her minor omission? She says that her husband was under contract to give a lecture at the hotel and she didn't want to be separated from him.

Mugger's Surprise

The life of crime is full of surprises. One might assume that a person in a wheelchair would not be the victim of a robbery. After all, there is some honor among criminals. But Deron Johnson did not adhere to that ethos and tried to snatch a chain off the neck of Margaret Johnson (no relation) as the fifty-six-year-old sat in her wheelchair.

Margaret may have been surprised by the attempted mugging, but Deron got the bigger surprise when Margaret pulled out a .357 pistol and shot him in the elbow. Deron was taken to the hospital, treated for a single gunshot wound, and then charged with attempted robbery. Margaret was also taken to the hospital suffering from minor injuries. She was treated and released.

As for Margaret's view of things, it's pretty cut-and-dried: "Somebody tried to mug me, and I shot him."

Another Saturday Night and I Ain't Got Nobody

Police in Wisconsin received a call of suspicious activity at the St. Charles Catholic Cemetery in Cassville on September 2, 2006. When they arrived, they found Dustin Radke and twins Nicholas and Alexander Grunke, all twenty years old, trying to dig up the body of Laura Tennessen, a twenty-year-old woman who had been killed in a motorcycle crash. The three had seen her obituary and decided to dig up the body to have sex with the corpse.

The police placed them under arrest but a judge dismissed attempted sexual assault charges because there was no law in Wisconsin outlawing necrophilia. (Apparently, Wisconsin legislators assumed that no one would be so disturbed as to contemplate such an act. These legislators never met the Grunke twins and Dustin Radke.) The three were charged with criminal damage to property and the alleged attempt to break into the burial vault.

MSNBC, obviously in an effort to defend the assault on Western values, ran the following headline in connection with their necrophilia story: "Just because it's not illegal, doesn't mean it's OK."

There are crimes that follow a person around during his life. For these three, this crime will certainly not be forgotten soon. Somewhere on some street corner in Wisconsin, a person is turning to his friend and saying "You see that guy over there? Isn't he the one . . ."

Criminals Caught with Their Pants Down

Stories all over the country confirm this truism: Before you go out to commit a crime, you'd better know how to dress.

James Green of Detroit, Michigan, stole a half-dozen DVDs and fled on his bicycle. When the police gave chase, he abandoned his bicycle and ran. He got tripped up twice by his baggy pants. He finally kicked off his pants and shoes and jumped a fence but was eventually captured by the police. He pleaded guilty to retail fraud and got a thirty-day sentence, all on account of baggy pants.

A mugger in Chattanooga, Tennessee, snatched Vicky Chandler's pocketbook and fled. He ran very fast but as he bolted, his loose khaki pants fell down. He reached down to hold them up and discarded the pocketbook.

Denny Fuhrman, a police officer from Lynnwood, Washington, was escorting a prisoner to his patrol car when the prisoner bolted. His baggy blue jeans

fell down around his ankles and he tumbled into traffic. The criminal wiggled out of his jeans and fled to a nearby mall. Officer Fuhrman put out the following description: "White male, running, no pants, in handcuffs." The man was arrested by a passerby in front of a JC Penney store.

College Athlete's Tomfoolery: "I Could Kick Myself"

Mitch Cozad, the second-string kicker for the University of Northern Colorado, decided to try to become a first-string kicker in the oddest of ways: He stabbed Rafael Mendoza, the first-string kicker, in Mendoza's kicking leg. The attack took place in the parking lot of Mendoza's apartment complex. The stab wound was three to five inches in depth and one inch in width.

Cozad escaped from the scene on foot and then got into his car in a nearby store parking lot. An eyewitness saw Cozad remove tape from the front and rear license plates, revealing his vanity tags, which read "8-KIKR." The car was registered to Cozad's mother.

Cozad had asked a teammate for directions to Mendoza's apartment complex, claiming to be looking for an apartment.

Cozad was cut from the team, suspended from school, arrested, and charged with assault. He was convicted of assault in the second degree and received a sentence of seven years.

Syracuse Sting: The Cop Pretending to Be a John; the Prostitute Pretending to Be a Cop

The police often pretend to be someone else in order to catch the bad guy (or gal). A Syracuse, New York, police officer pretended to be a john (a man looking to retain the services of a prostitute) as he drove in an area known for prostitution. He met up with a woman who got into his car, and they began haggling over the price for sex.

The alleged prostitute asked the Syracuse undercover cop if he was indeed a cop, and he said he was not. The prostitute then told him that *she* was a cop. She pulled out a two-way radio and handcuffs and barked into the radio, "Move in!"

The undercover officer was not fooled by the scam. He forced the female cop impostor from the car and, pretending to be a female, spoke into the two-way

radio in an effort to identify the person on the other line. The police arrested Lisa Greene and her accomplice, Elena Irwin. Greene was charged with criminal impersonation, prostitution, and other charges. The police believed that the two women were trying to rob people or extort money.

Cybercrime:
How to Break into Jail

There are some people who seem to want to break *into* jail. Jon Houston Elpp, thirty-nine, of Novato, California, appears to be such a person.

Elpp was on trial for a burglary involving computers. During the middle of the trial, he was caught stealing computers from the courthouse. Elpp pleaded guilty to three charges with a promised sentence of up to five years in jail.

In a jailhouse interview, Elpp said that he stole the computers "for personal reasons." He said, "I needed help, and I didn't know how to ask for help. And I guess, in my crazy way, that was my way of asking for help. Help with my drug problems, help with my sanity."

Designated Driver Drives Himself to Jail

Robert DeRosa, fifty-one, is indeed a true friend. His pal Kenneth Tulaba was arrested for DWI, and DeRosa drove to the Long Island police precinct to check up on him. The only problem was that DeRosa himself was drunk. Police saw DeRosa exit the car in the precinct parking lot, appearing intoxicated. He refused to submit to a chemical test and was arrested.

A Coffee Break You'd Like to Miss as Government Employee Goes Postal

In an Austin Powers movie, Austin mistakes a stool sample for coffee and he complains that the sample tastes like s–t. For some postal workers in Akron, Ohio, such a scenario was no laughing matter.

Something about their coffee was not right. The workers demanded an investigation, but nothing came of the probe. Taking matters into their own hands, the workers installed a video camera in the break room and in July 2005 taped Thomas Shaheen, fifty, pouring urine into the coffeepot on two occasions.

Jene Jackson, a coworker, was shocked: "We can't believe Thomas would even stoop to this level for his own personal revenge. He would sit in the same room with people and watch them drink his sick little brew and think nothing of it."

Shaheen pleaded guilty to two misdemeanor counts of tainting the office coffee. He was sentenced to six

months in a jail work-release program and ordered to reimburse his coworkers for $1,200 to cover the cost of making the secret video.

Shaheen did not give a motive. His lawyer, Paul Adamson, said that he was frustrated about his work. Shaheen, who had worked at the post office vehicle maintenance facility for thirteen years, was fired as a result of this incident.

THE MAGIC KINGDOM OF FRAUD AND CRIME

Mickey Mouse and Fred Flintstone
Vote for Ralph Nader

The Pennsylvania Supreme Court ordered Ralph Nader and his running mate, Peter Miguel Camejo, to pay more than eighty thousand dollars in expenses for a lawsuit that challenged their nominating papers and kept them off the 2004 ballot.

The court ruled that there was fraud and deception in the petition drive. Nearly two-thirds of the fifty-one thousand signatures were disqualified. The lower court found that thousands of names were created at random. Among the names were Fred Flintstone and Mickey Mouse.

The Pennsylvania Supreme Court upheld the trial court's charging Nader and Camejo with transcription and stenography costs and handwriting expert

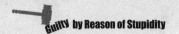

fees. Justice Sandra Schultz Newman, writing for the majority, stated, "Given the magnitude of the fraud and deception implicated in [their] signature-gathering efforts, their claim that the Commonwealth Court acted in an unjust and unconstitutional fashion by assessing transcription and stenography costs does not pass the straight-face test."

Goofy Bank Robber Nabbed

Jo Walker, thirty-seven, of Patchogue, New York, was arrested for robbing two banks, one in East Meadow, New York, and the other one in Merrick, New York. She had a unique MO: She would stash her money in a black bag that had pictures of Mickey Mouse, Goofy, Pluto, and other Disney stars.

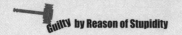
It's a Sick World after All...

An Illinois judge initially gave Frank Atherton, forty-six, permission to travel to Florida. Nothing wrong with that, right? Wrong. The only problem with that was that Atherton planned to visit Disney World and he faced charges of sexually assaulting two girls and one boy, all under the age of thirteen. Associate judge R. Craig Sahlstrom claimed he was unaware of the fact that Atherton was going to Disney. He ordered the defendant's lawyer to contact Atherton, who had already left for Florida, and tell him not to go to the theme park.

Atherton's lawyer thought there was nothing wrong with letting Atherton take that trip to Disney with his family. He pointed out that the defendant is presumed innocent until found guilty. Atherton had previously served time in prison for armed robbery, burglary, and theft, according to court records.

Have no fear about Atherton. After all, his lawyer called him and told him not to go to Disney.

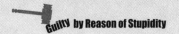

Another Illinois judge, Amy J. St. Eve, permitted a major figure in a terrorism investigation, Chicago grocer Muhammed Salah, to take a trip to Walt Disney World. Salah had been acquitted of a racketeering conspiracy in connection with laundering and delivering money to Hamas, a terrorist group, but was convicted of lying about his connections to Hamas in a civil lawsuit.

The Life of a Cocaine Smuggler: From Big Hair to the Big House

A U.S. tourist with a woman's beehive hairstyle was arrested in Ireland when it was discovered that she had concealed about a kilo of cocaine in black packages in her hair. The Web site Breitbart.com had a headline to remember: "It's dandruff, madame?"

Honest Cop Fines Himself for Passing School Bus with Flashing Lights

Police chief Richard Knoebel accidentally passed a school bus with flashing lights in Kewaskum, Wisconsin. The police chief wrote himself a ticket for $235, gave himself four points on his license, and immediately paid the fine.

He did not make a big deal about it. In fact, the incident happened in September 2006 but did not make it into the newspaper until February 2007. Although Chief Knoebel did not pass the bus on purpose, he thought it would be helpful for the public to know he gave himself a ticket. "If it brings notice to people that they should be stopping for school buses, I don't mind the notoriety," he said.

Sword-Wielding Neighbor to the Rescue; Oops, It Was Just a Porn Movie

An Oconomowoc, Wisconsin, man claims he broke into his neighbor's house wielding a sword because he thought he heard the screams of a woman being raped. James Van Iveren says he was listening to music in his apartment when he heard the woman's screams emanating from a nearby apartment. He took his thirty-nine-inch sword and forced his way into the apartment of Brad Stieghorst, damaging the door frame and lock in the process. He demanded that Stieghorst lead him to the woman in distress.

In fact, there was a logical explanation for Van Iveren's conclusion that he needed to save a rape victim: Stieghorst was watching a pornographic DVD. Stieghorst led Van Iveren through the apartment, opening the closets to show he was alone. Van Iveren said, "Now I feel stupid. This really is nothing, nothing but a mistake."

Van Iveren was charged with misdemeanor trespassing while using a dangerous weapon and criminal damage to property. His sword was confiscated. Stieghorst denied that his pornographic movie sounded like a damsel in distress. He said he was watching an adult DVD in Spanish called *Casa de Culo.* He said the movie had no screaming in it, so Van Iveren could not have thought a woman was in danger. "It's all in Spanish, and I don't understand a word of it," he said. "I only bought it for the hot chicks."

The story was widely reported, but what the press missed was the fact that Van Iveren was well-known to the Oconomowoc police. He was once accused of impersonating an undercover investigator to avoid being evicted from his apartment.

"You see, I am a lieutenant in the Wisconsin State Patrol," Van Iveren wrote in a letter to his landlord in 2000, asking the landlord to delay the eviction against his mother and him. "I am very strongly insisting that you do this so that you don't compromise my current investigation or do any further harm to my mother."

A Challenge to Those with Common Sense: Try to Figure This One Out

Judith Clark is currently serving seventy-five years for acting as a getaway driver in a 1981 Brink's armored truck robbery in which a guard and two police officers were killed. Her codefendants included Kathy Boudin, a former member of a radical organization. Boudin was paroled in 2003.

At the time of the trial, Clark insisted on representing herself rather than having the benefit of a court-appointed lawyer. She then insisted that she remain in her cell outside the court while the trial was proceeding. The judge permitted her to represent herself and also acceded to her request to not appear in the courtroom.

Enter federal district court judge Shira Scheindlin, who ordered a new trial, claiming that the trial judge should have appointed a lawyer for Clark, even though she did not want a lawyer and chose to stay in her cell.

If your head is spinning trying to figure out the logic in this decision, don't worry. You are perfectly normal.

Peter Paige, a Brink's security guard, was killed at the Nanuet Mall during the heist that netted $1.8 million. Two Rockland County policemen were also killed as the gang of robbers tried to avoid a roadblock. As the two officers lay wounded, another officer ordered the defendants to put their weapons down. Clark reached for a handgun in the car.

"No one held a gun to Judith Clark's head and told her to not attend the trial or have an attorney. Now twenty-four years later, she's claiming her rights were violated. There is no merit to her case," said Tim Connolly, a retired NYPD officer and president of the Rockland County Shields fraternal police organization.

"She had a free choice and chose not to have an attorney," Richard Brightenback, a Rockland County resident, told the *Journal News*. "If the judge forced a lawyer on her, she would have appealed."

A three-judge panel of a federal appeals court unanimously reversed Scheindlin's bizarre ruling. They said that Clark's claim that she had been deprived

of her Sixth Amendment rights (the right to counsel) had "no merit whatsoever" since the choices that she made to represent herself and avoid the courtroom were her own.

I Saw Mommy Groping Santa Claus

It is a tough job to play Santa at the mall nowadays. Pity the poor man who had this job at the Danbury, Connecticut, mall in December 2007. He suffered the ultimate insult. A thirty-three-year-old woman sat on Santa's lap, and apparently having a thing for full-figured bearded men dressed in red, she groped Santa. Santa told a reporter, "I don't know what the deal was. It was just bizarre." What was equally bizarre is why Santa Claus complained about the holiday groping. The security officer at the mall leaped into action, calling the Danbury police to arrest this person who posed a danger to Santa Clauses all over America.

When the police arrived, they had no problem tracking down thirty-three-year-old Sandrama Lamy. She was trying to escape on crutches. The sixty-five-year-old Santa was apparently upset by the unwanted touching.

"Santa Tim" Connaghan, president of RealSantas. com, a company that trains hundreds of Santas, said he had never heard of a similar incident.

"I've had some very nice ladies sit on my lap," he said. "Once in a while they'll say, 'I hope Mrs. Claus isn't going to be upset.' You have to be discreet and kind and say, 'Oh, no, she'll be OK. You can sit here, but only for one photo.'"

Lamy was sentenced to two years' probation. If she completes probation, her record will be wiped clean. She was ordered to keep away from the Danbury mall.

Two Boobs on North Carolina Court Deny Woman Second Implant

Penny M. Rumple Richardson was in a car accident that caused unusual damages: a rippling and decrease in the size of her breast implants. She sued to replace the two implants. An expert testified to the damage to the left implant and the rippling to the right implant. The three-judge panel all agreed that breast implants are covered under workers' compensation law. After all, implants are "a prosthetic device that functions as a part of the body." However, two of the judges decided to award her only one breast implant.

James Wynn Jr., the sole dissenting judge, recognized something that was pointed out in Woody Allen's *Everything You Wanted to Know About Sex But Were Afraid to Ask:* Breasts usually travel in pairs. He wanted to give Richardson both implants to make sure that the implants were "symmetrical and evenly matched."

One thing is for sure: Two of the three judges on the panel are boobs.

Missile Attack at Laramie, Wyoming, School; Cops Arrest Thirteen-Year-Old Homegrown Terrorists

If you think the fear of terror is only real in New York, Chicago, Washington, D.C., and L.A., then you haven't visited Laramie, Wyoming, where the police charged three thirteen-year-olds with an infraction of a city ordinance prohibiting the hurling of missiles. The missiles involved were not the shoulder-launched rocket-propelled grenades that endanger and harm our troops in Afghanistan and Iraq. They were missiles whose prime ingredient was made in Idaho: French fries. The three Laramie Junior High School students were charged with hurling missiles for their participation in a food fight.

Laramie Junior High's principal and a police officer had warned students during an assembly the day before the missile launch that if they engaged in a food

fight, they would suffer the consequences. There was no indication from Laramie police whether the crime was more serious if the fries were fried in trans fat.

Dead Man Rolling
on Streets of New York

David Daloia and James O'Hare, both sixty-five years old, had a unique way of trying to cash sixty-six-year-old Virgilio Cintron's $355 social security check. You see, Cintron was dead. The two geniuses undoubtedly worried that a check casher might ask them if they had Cintron's permission to cash the check, so they came up with an ingenious plan: They put Cintron's corpse on a desk chair and rolled it to a Pay-O-Matic store in New York City.

NYPD detective Travis Rapp noticed the corpse from inside a restaurant and called 911. When asked by the check casher where Cintron was, the two men pointed outside the store, where Cintron sat dead on the chair. When the two men started to wheel Cintron inside, a crowd gathered around. Part of the problem with the scheme was that the chair had no arms, so poor Cintron was flopping around during his trip down the sidewalk.

Cintron had died of natural causes, so the two clever criminals were charged only with attempted forgery, criminal possession of a forged instrument, and petit larceny. After being released on bail, O'Hare and Daloia and told a *Daily News* reporter that they believed their friend was alive when they wheeled him through Manhattan. "Of course, we didn't know he was dead," Daloia said. "He looked like that every . . . morning."

"Everybody misunderstands," said O'Hare, who was Cintron's roommate. "I love him, and I miss him."

"Kiss My A–s"
Worth Another Ninety Days
in Judge's Eyes

We are guaranteed freedom of speech by our Constitution but sometimes exercising free speech will cost you your freedom. For Judith Law, who had violated probation on her grand larceny conviction, she learned that lesson by insulting the judge. Judge Diane Goodstein sentenced Law to five years' incarceration. When signing the probation revocation order, Judith Law insulted the judge. She wrote: "Kiss My A–s." That suggestion added another ninety days to Law's sentence. The South Carolina Court of Appeals upheld the ninety-day sentence for insulting the judge.

Credit Card Thief Is Released on Bail When He Recites Twenty-third Psalm

Eric Hine, a Cincinnati, Ohio, man, was arrested for buying goods in a drugstore with a stolen credit card. When he came to court, his lawyer argued that he was a churchgoer. The judge was skeptical and asked the defendant to recite the Twenty-third Psalm. Much to the surprise and entertainment of the court spectators, the thief said all six verses perfectly.

The judge was impressed and released the defendant on a ten-thousand-dollar appearance bond. His church better keep an eye on him when they pass around the poor plate.

When Nature Calls, How Much Is Enough?

People have different viewpoints on how much toilet paper is enough to get the job done. For Kansas inmates, four rolls of toilet paper a month isn't enough; for Sheryl Crow, one square a sitting does the trick.

The Hutchinson Correctional Facility in Kansas limits toilet paper to four rolls per inmate per month or on an "as-needed" basis. How and who determines what is "as needed" is wisely not spelled out. Carl Kennedy, a Hutchinson inmate, wrote a letter to the *Hutchinson News* to complain: "Some take it for granted. But in here it's part of a safeguard for widespread infections. We use it to blow our noses, clean sinks, toilets, and tables."

The inmates should be grateful that Sheryl Crow, entertainer and environmentalist, is not their warden. Crow proposed a limitation on the number of squares per sitting to stave off a global warming catastrophe. She suggested "only one square per restroom visit, except, of course, on those pesky occasions where two to three could be required." The warden looks kinder than Crow.

D.C. Judge Takes Laundry to Cleaners Over Lost Pants

Roy Pearson, a Washington, D.C., lawyer and administrative judge, must have some sentimental attachment to his pants. He took a pair to a dry cleaner, where they were lost. In a rational, sane society, the dry cleaner would pay for the lost pants and life would go on. Pearson filed suit for the pants.

In spite of offers by the owners, Jin Nam Chung and Ki Chung, to settle the lawsuit for amounts between $3,000 and $12,000, the plaintiff sued for $67 million. The genius judge's theory behind his attempted grand larceny: two signs that say "Satisfaction Guaranteed" and "Same Day Service." Since the spoiled judge claims he got neither, he says that he is entitled to $1,500 per day, because the signs amount to fraud. (The fine for consumer fraud is $1,500 per day.)

The Chungs were supported by Sherman Joyce, president of the American Tort Reform Association, who wrote a letter to the appointment committee urging them to revoke Pearson's reappointment as administrative judge. And a National Labor Relations Board chief administrative law judge wrote a letter to the *Washington Post* saying, "Any bar to which Pearson belongs to [should] immediately disbar him and the District [should] remove him from his position as an administrative law judge."

It would be quite interesting to appear before the Honorable Judge Pearson to see if the justice he dispenses is anywhere as bizarre as the lawsuit he brought.

Pearson most likely had his own reasons for his idiotic lawsuit, including a recent divorce that had left only one to two thousand dollars in his bank account. The press was all over the lawsuit, and fortunately Judge Judith Bartnoff decided Pearson was entitled to nothing and then did something even better—she ordered Pearson to pay the Chungs' court costs.

At the end of the day, it was Pearson who was caught with his pants down.

Driving Four-Ton Zamboni While Drunk Is Okay in New Jersey

Zamboni operator John Peragallo was grooming the ice in the Mennen Sports Arena in Morristown, New Jersey, while a bit tipsy. He was traveling very fast and nearly smacked into the boards. When a fellow employee told the police, the police arrested Peragallo. He blew a .12 blood-alcohol level. Peragallo had a shot of Sambuca with his breakfast coffee along with two Valium pills. Although the legal limit for driving in New Jersey is .08, superior court judge Joseph Falcone exonerated Peragallo, since, he said, a Zamboni does not ride on highways and does not carry passengers.

CELEBRITY CRIME: LIFESTYLES OF THE STUPID AND FAMOUS

Evander Holyfield, aka Evan Fields, Can't Fool the Steroid Police

Sports Illustrated's Web site reported that a patient who purchased steroids did so under the name Evan Fields. Coincidentally, Evan Fields had a similar address and the same date of birth as Evander Holyfield.

When reporters called the telephone number associated with these prescriptions, Evander Holyfield answered the phone. Holyfield issued a statement through his promoter that said, "I do not use steroids. I have never used steroids."

If Evander Holyfield or Evan Fields wishes to sue me because of this blurb, please note that it was not written by Joel Seidemann; it was written by someone else: Joe Seidema.

SCHOOLHOUSE ROCK: LEGAL LUNACY IN HALLS OF LEARNING

Student Moons Teacher, Then Sues

Tyler Tillung, an eighteen-year-old Florida high school student, mooned his teacher for not allowing him into the school's lip-synch show, which was already full. He was suspended for six days and reassigned to a new school.

Wanting to graduate with his Palm Harbor University High class and complete his final season on the varsity baseball season, Tillung sued to get back into the school.

His lawyer, B. Edwin Johnson (beware of people with first initials in their names) noted, "We're talking about his graduation. That's an important event in a guy's life. . . . This kid deserves a break." Yeah, that's right. A guy who mooned his teacher is concerned about his graduation.

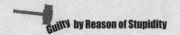

Principal Herman "Doc" Allen described the mooning as "disgusting" and the teacher as "traumatized." Apparently, Tillung is not an ordinary a–hole.

Student Sues University of Massachusetts Over Lousy Grade

Brian Marquis, a fifty-year-old University of Massachusetts student, is suing the school because he got a C in philosophy, which could hurt his chances of getting into law school. Yes, it does sound very absurd, but check this out; the story gets weirder.

Marquis initially earned a 92.1 in the course. However, a teaching assistant redrew the grading scale "to make grades more representative of student performance," which turned Marquis's 92.1 percent into 84 percent.

At the University of Massachusetts, 84 percent can produce a grade between A- and C, depending on the professor's preferences, according to the school newspaper, the *Daily Collegian*.

You don't know who to root for in this one.

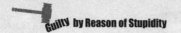

Indiana Student Gets Suspended Because He Had a Pot to Piss In

An Indiana middle school teacher woke up and smelled the coffee, but the odor was not exactly Colombian coffee beans. The school's investigation discovered that an eighth grader had put urine in the teacher's coffee pot. More urine was found in the student's locker.

The school got tough. The student was suspended and may be expelled. Dilynn Phelps, in a letter to parents, noted, "this type of student behavior will not be tolerated. No student will be permitted to deliberately attempt to cause bodily harm to any other student, teacher, or staff member."

Peeping Tom for Roommate

In Manchester, Connecticut, two females and three males were roommates. The arrangement seemed to be fine, until a male roommate noticed there was a bottle of shampoo in a shower basket that never

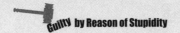
seemed to move. Upon further examination, he saw that wires were sticking out of the bottle. He called the police, who discovered a tiny camera in the bottle that recorded images through a peephole.

The police questioned twenty-five-year-old Steven Thibodeau, who at first told them he was filming himself in the shower to monitor an abnormality. (Great story, Steve!) After being given a polygraph, Thibodeau admitted to filming his two female roommates in the shower. He faced fifteen counts of voyeurism and one count of evidence tampering. Superior court judge Raymond Norko said, "This one is totally off the wall."

Police: James Brown's Height Dispute Causes Shooting

Dan Guilley Jr. was charged with assault after shooting his friend David James Brooks while at another friend's house. Guiley, seventy, argued with Brooks over the height of James Brown, the godfather of soul. (Known to wear lifts, Brown died on December 25, 2006, of heart failure.)

Guilley shot Brooks, sixty-two, twice in the abdomen. Brooks then went to his car and shot at Guilley but missed.

Both Alabama residents went to the police station to report the incident. The police did not believe that alcohol was a factor. (If it were, that would have explained it.)

Fake Cop Sets Up Fake Police Station

Henry Terry of Holbrook, New York, really wanted to be a cop. To that end, he ordered all sorts of badges, uniforms, handcuffs, and other law enforcement paraphernalia over the Internet. Equipping his car with lights and a siren, Terry would stop motorists on the road and take suspects to his own personal police station he had set up in an office building in Long Island. The building directory listed Terry's office as "New York Enforcement Asset Recovery Bureau's District 2 Operations." Terry had a name tag that read "Cpl. H. Terry, Unit Supervisor."

When Terry brought traffic violators back to the "station," he photocopied their identification, just like real cops do. According to the district attorney, Terry got some victims to give him cash in exchange for their release.

Terry's impersonation ended when he convinced the owner of an SUV to give him the use of the

SUV in an undercover operation. He then swapped that SUV and $600 for a different vehicle. He was caught and charged with grand larceny and criminal impersonation.

Jail Time for Man Who Faked Retardation

Pete Costello, a twenty-eight-year-old Vancouver, Washington, man, pleaded guilty to defrauding the government of close to sixty thousand dollars. Costello began receiving disability payments when he was eight years old by pretending to be retarded. When he appeared at the social security office, he picked at his face, slouched, and appeared uncommunicative.

He had been taught to feign mental retardation by his mother, Rosie, who coached both Pete and her daughter in the scam.

Costello got caught when he got a traffic ticket in Vancouver and acted normally when he fought the ticket in court.